INTIMACY IN GOD

Growing Deeper in Him

by

Glenn N. Collier

ISBN-13: 978-1475134810
ISBN-10: 1475134819

Published by
Glenn Collier Ministries
P.O. Box 490054
Lawrenceville, Ga. 30019

Visit our Website at
www.glenncollier.com
www.newharvester.org

Scripture quotations marked NLT are taken from the Holy Bible, New Living Translation of the Bible. Copyright © 1996, 2004. Used by permission of Tyndale House Publishers Inc., Carol Stream, Illinois 60188. All rights are reserved.

Scripture quotations noted "KJV" are taken from The Holy Bible, KING JAMES VERSION.

CONTENTS

INTRODUCTION

By Bishop Glenn Collier

My purpose for writing this book is to help you carry God's presence and His heart by developing greater *Intimacy In God*. I encourage you to read this book with the right motive to let the Holy Spirit melt your heart and stir you to fall on your knees, and increasingly pray to know God's heart deeper and more intimately. I pray that you would never view this book with the attitude of knowing about God by head knowledge alone, but focus on your own greater *Intimacy In God*.

It is God's heart that you have precious *Intimacy* to pray with the right spirit and right heart and get into that place of one purpose to know God more fully. Then, you can obey Him, enjoy His favor, and be set apart by God's presence and glory.

Intimacy in God will stir and inspire you to become a flame of fire, understand the price to live in God's presence, flow in the anointing, and have God's power flowing through you as a clean vessel to shake your city and nation with God's glory. Become familiar with the presence, will, mind, attitude, and heart of God and daily live in His presence—the abiding glory.

Man of God, *Intimacy in God* is the first and most important thing you can do to take you into your godly position as a priest of your home, church, or ministry. Then, you can walk with purity and Holiness, and be a carrier of God's presence. Learn how to watch over your house, see things in the spirit regarding what is going on, and cover your family. If you want to be able to see the things that God sees in your children, spouse, or loved ones, and speak life and not death to them, this is your season to have greater *Intimacy In God.*

Woman of God, I encourage you to develop increased *Intimacy In God* so you can be a living testimony as a godly woman and carrier of God's glory. If married, learn how to intercede for your spouse to become the godly priest of your home. Go after God's glory with purity, godliness, and Holiness of heart. If you are single, pray for your family, loved ones, and church to have purity and Holiness of heart. Step into your rightful place to be used mightily for His glory.

Young person, you can impact your whole generation by godliness, purity, and Holiness of heart through deeper *Intimacy In God*! The devil wants to steal your purity and defile you with uncleanness because he hates you and is afraid of God's glory and does not want you to have God's power in your life.

Intimacy In God is the most important thing you need to set your eyes upon the Lord, hear God, avoid traps and snares, and be delivered out of what the world sets before you!

No matter what has happened, now is the time to chase after God's glory, and He will change you and move you into your destiny. God will put His name and stamp of approval upon you and the whole world will know that you belong to Jesus and His glory will flow through you.

In every situation, through the Word of God and truth you have learned, learn how to walk it out in your life through *Intimacy In God.* This is your season to have new levels and depths in the realms of God's presence. When you have *Intimacy In God*, you will understand the importance of God's presence that is more valuable than any person or treasure on earth, and knowing Him as your number one goal in life.

When you have the right spirit to know God, be filled with Holiness, and continually keep this focus, then, godliness will lead you to go forward through any life experience and God's glory will protect you from behind. As you stay in God's presence, no evil can stand against you because you are carrying God's glory. You will not need to protect yourself from behind; you will not need to be watching over your shoulder, or worry what the enemy is trying to do against you. Your godliness will be leading you and His glory will protect you from behind.

God's Word promises that when you have the right spirit to give yourself completely over to Him through *Intimacy In God*, He will speedily respond when you call on His name.

When having *Intimacy In God*, you will be able to hear God, know how God thinks and responds to things, and how He lives. Then, you will have His abiding presence and supernatural glory with demonstration of power flowing in and through you to bring people to Jesus.

Many have a wrong spirit to seek God only for things. However, if they chase after *Intimacy In God*, they will seek first the Kingdom of God and His righteousness by intimate relationship to know Him in such a way and stay in that place. Then, God will cause all the things they need to chase after them.

As you pursue greater *Intimacy In God*, you will not be led by your rational thinking to do things your way, but will continually seek God to know Him so you can do things His way. By doing this, your godliness will lead you into doing the will of God and fulfilling your God-ordained destiny.

Wonderful are the ways of the Lord and *Intimacy In God* is your blessed destiny! Go after God until you know you have His heart and He has all of yours. Greater Intimacy In God is my earnest prayer for you.

CHAPTER 1
GOING AFTER
THE PRESENCE &
GLORY OF GOD

"Seek the Kingdom of God above all else, and live righteously, and he will give you everything you need."

Matthew 6:33 (NLT)

Knowing how to go after the wonderful power and glory of God's presence is the most crucial thing for every believer! When you know how to do this, you will be able to obey God's call for your life and not become distracted by other things.

Many are not aware of the things that can drown out God's voice and hinder them from fulfilling their first word and call that God told them to do for His purpose. They were not able to go any further in God because they did not understand the need to pursue God's presence as first in their lives.

I want to challenge you to obey the call that God has put on your life and you can do it today by going after His presence. Jonah tried to run, but he could never run from God's presence, His call, and the word God gave him to do. After a great storm, he faced his final decision to obey God.

I pray that this chapter will stir you to know the importance of going after God's presence as first and foremost in your life. In order to go after the presence of God, you must discern three types of storms in your life.

1

Jonah tried to run from the call but ultimately, God brought Him back into His will. It is crucial that you discern the nature and purpose of storms that lead to obedience and perfect you in His image.

Storms that develop godly character bring us into greater levels of His presence. Storms can bring glory to the awesome name of Jesus when they are storms that impact and transform the lives of people around us.

It is God's heart for you to have greater and more wonderful intimacy with Him, and to know Him more and more. You can start today; it is not too late! If you disobeyed or ignored God's call, today is the day you can get back into God's plan and purpose for your life. You can do it by going after His presence. The purpose of this chapter is to challenge you to go after intimacy of God's presence and obey His call on your life.

You Know God is Real
By Experiencing
The Power of His Presence

To have intimacy in God, you must go after God's presence and glory. When His presence manifests, God is not just encouraging your heart—He is changing your life. He is after His image. He is after perfecting you. God desires that you look just like Him. Ultimately, that is what God is after. He is the one that moves your heart to know that He is with you.

Let me share various ways God can move your heart to know He is with you. When you fellowship with believers, it maybe just one nugget, one thing, one moment, one prayer that is prayed, one song that is sung, or a testimony that someone has given, which moves your heart to know that God is with you.

2

It may be just one thing that moves your heart to a place that you know beyond question that God is there with you. Therefore, it is not just by faith, but also by knowledge of the power of His presence that you know God is with you. This is important in your life.

Right Now, You Can
Live in His Presence!

It is important that you continually have the Lord's presence on your job and everywhere you go. On our jobs, we do not want to be found as people of religion. We want to be found as people of His presence. I talk much about His presence because ultimately, it is where I am going to live and God is preparing us to live in His presence.

However, God is not waiting for us to get to Heaven; we are to live in His presence right now! In order to live in God's presence, we must want to be familiar with His presence, will, mind, attitude, and heart. This must be the reason why we want intimacy in God.

Religion is Boring &
Produces No Change of Heart—
God's Presence is Fresh & Changes Hearts

You must want intimacy with God because you need His presence that changes your heart. Religion is boring and produces no real change of heart. Our nation is seeing too much religion and not enough of God's presence.

People have sought after religion, which is a hard thing to break when a person is doing something repeatedly, systematically, and all the time. It is hard to break that habit. Religious people are used to the routine of outward ritual performance, traditions of men, and religious activities that have no real life. It is hard to break that habit or mold of doing things the same way and not allowing God to do it His way. Religion brings bondage; God's presence brings life—real life!

I believe that our nation has not changed as much as it could be changed because it takes the presence of God to change things and situations. God's presence delivers and changes things. God is fresh all the time. His presence is always fresh and exciting! There is nothing stale about God. He is never stale. No one can run from God's presence. In His presence, He can move us to our knees—to a place of brokenness and total dependency on Him.

You Cannot Run
From God's Presence

We cannot run from His presence and God has many ways of moving us to our knees, a place of separation where we are set apart by God. *"You can be sure of this: The Lord set apart the godly for himself"* (Psalms 4:3 NLT).

The Bible tells us about Jonah's disobedience and that he could not run from God's presence. God gives Jonah a message and he tries to escape from God's presence. The scriptures do not say that he argued with God or even thought about it.

As soon as God gave him the message, Jonah got up immediately and went in the other direction. Think about that! The scripture says, *"The LORD gave this message to Jonah son of Amittai: 'Get up and go to the great city of Nineveh. Announce my judgment against it because I have seen how wicked its people are.' But Jonah got up and went in the opposite direction to get away from the LORD. He*

4

went down to the port of Joppa, where he found a ship leaving for Tarshish. He bought a ticket and went on board, hoping to escape from the LORD by sailing to Tarshish" (Jonah 1:1-3 NLT).

Some People Try to Run
From God & the Call

Many times, when we hear the Word of the Lord or hear a call of God, we will leave things running from the call. Some people will not obey God's call and try to run from it. They even leave homes and lands running from the call like Jonah did. The Bible says that Jonah had a call from God. The Word of God was placed on him, and instead of leaving everything for the call, he left everything to get away from the call. He was trying to get away from the Word of the Lord. It is amazing to me that he would leave and that very same day, he bought a ticket, went out to the shipyard, boarded a ship and sailed.

I wonder what responsibilities Jonah had that this man would hear the Word of God and immediately respond by going in the opposite direction. I wonder if he had a job or a family. Jonah is not the only one who has ever run from his call. Some believers have heard the Word of the Lord and responded the same way. They heard the Word of God and went in the opposite direction.

People Drown Out God's Voice
By Noise & Busyness

Let me tell you how people run from the call. They can run from the call by getting busy doing other things. If we get busy, it may just drown out the voice of the Lord. That is not how we should live. We need to run to obey God's voice and

5

call.

A person can drown out the voice of the Lord by noise and busyness. By going in another direction, not only can a person drown out God's call on his or her life or a call to preach, but also other things that God has spoken. Sometimes, it is drowned out by doing some good things and people will say that those things are honorable to the Lord, but they are not doing what He said to do.

If You Drown Out the Call, You are Hindering God's Purpose

In addition, when people drown out the voice and call of the Lord, many things will happen. It is not just drowning out the voice of the Lord, but it is also drowning out what He wants to accomplish. It is also drowning out what He wants to do.

If you have a "God said" in your heart, you must be careful not to drown out what He told you to do. If you have something that you can hold onto and rely on and you know without question that God said it, you must not drown out what God wants to accomplish.

Some People Are Comfortable With the Call Inside Them & They Are Sleeping

Some are comfortable with the call inside them and are not willing to step out and obey. We need to be willing to step out with obedience and not be like Jonah. Again, I think it is strange that Jonah had the call and everybody else on the ship was afraid, but Jonah was in the ship sleeping.

6

The Bible says, *"But the LORD hurled a powerful wind over the sea, causing a violent storm that threatened to break the ship apart. Fearing for their lives, the desperate sailors shouted to their gods for help and threw the cargo overboard to lighten the ship. But all this time Jonah was sound asleep down in the hold"* (Jonah 1:4-5 NLT).

Everyone else is afraid and saying, "Call upon your God. Even if it is not the real God, we want everybody to call upon their gods. We need help right now." Here is what they were really saying, "We want every man to get up and call upon his god." That was when they went down to get Jonah.

However, this man of God was comfortable with the call of God inside of him and asleep in the ship. The scripture says, *"So the captain went down after him. 'How can you sleep at a time like this?' he shouted. 'Get up and pray to your god! Maybe he will pay attention to us and spare our lives'"* (Jonah 1:6 NLT). Like many today, he was comfortable with the call of God inside of him and he was sleeping.

You Need to Recognize the Kind Of Storm You Are Going Through

Jonah was sleeping through the storm and was not taking the time to discern the cause of it. We must be able to discern the cause of the storm. It is very interesting that the captain and the sailors had knowledge of the fact that the storm was something unusual. It speaks that this was not a normal storm.

The reason this scripture is important is that all of us will go through storms in our lives. We need to be able to recognize what kind of storm we are going through and be able to discern that storm.

In spite of the sailors being unbelievers, they were able to discern that something unusual was happening and it was not a usual storm. They went down and told the man of God that he needed to get up and pray. It says, *"Then the crew cast lots to see which of them had offended the gods and caused the terrible storm. When they did this, the lots identified Jonah as the culprit"* (Jonah 1:7 NLT).

Disobedience Can Cause
Your Comfort to Turn Into A
Sudden Shaking & Awakening

If a person is comfortable with the call and that person is asleep, the results will not be a good place for him. You do not want to be in that situation where you are around a group of people who are saying, "Something is happening to us right now, and we don't know what's going on, but we're going to cast lots," and then that lot falls on you. That is not a good place to be.

Consequently, the lot fell on Jonah. The scripture says, *"'Why has this awful storm come down on us?' they demanded. 'Who are you? What is your line of work? What country are you from? What is your nationality?'"* (Jonah 1:8 NLT) Suddenly, this gets serious because they were trying to trace what was happening to their lives, and a desperate situation arose for Jonah.

A Desperate Situation May Arise &
You Will Have to Deal With It

At the same time, a desperate situation can arise in your life, which can expose that you are running from God and you are going to have to deal with it.

8

The Bible says that the storm was so fierce that the sailors were trying to trace this thing. They traced it to Jonah and they wanted to know what he did. Something had happened that Jonah had not dealt with and it was following him.

In like manner, if running from a word from the Lord, and a person is not dealing with that, it will follow him. Suddenly he may be exposed so he can deal with it. In his life, Jonah came to the time that he had to publicly deal with it.

Look how Jonah dealt with it. The answer that Jonah told them was, *"... I am a Hebrew, and I worship the LORD, the God of heaven, who made the sea and the land"* (Jonah 1:9 NLT).

In short, he was running from God, boarded the ship and they asked him where he was going. That is interesting. Evidently, he declared, "I'm running from God." They knew it because he had already announced that he was running from God.

Look what happened next. The scripture says that his response made them terrified. *"The sailors were terrified when they heard this, for he had already told them he was running away from the LORD. 'Oh, why did you do it?' they groaned"* (Verse 10 NLT).

In other words, one may not be in the position he is supposed to be because he is running from God. At the present, it may not be outwardly shown, but when God gives you an assignment, circumstances may suddenly arise to move you into God's first purpose and plan for you.

We must understand the heart of God to move us into the right place and position He intended.

Until You Change, God May Not Allow
You or the Situations Around You to Rest

In essence, things in your life may suddenly happen that will cause you to make a change to get back into God's first plan for your life. With Jonah, things began to suddenly develop that God would not allow. What was inside Jonah was so serious to God that He would not allow him to rest, or the people around him to rest, nor the situations that were storming around him. He could not rest until it was changed into what God ordained to happen from the beginning.

Change was about to happen for Jonah. The Bible records the moment Jonah had to make a decision to change the situation around him and he had no choice to stay in the same place. It says, *"Since the storm was getting worse all the time, they asked him, 'What should we do to you to stop this storm'"* (Jonah 1:11 NLT)?

Therefore, to stop a storm, sometimes you might be sacrificed. The Bible says that the sailors asked Jonah what they should do to stop the storm. The scripture tells us that Jonah said it like this, *"Throw me into the sea ... and it will become calm again. I know that this terrible storm is all my fault"* (Jonah 1:12 NLT). Finally, Jonah acknowledged that the storm was his fault.

Some Storms Stop
When You Obey God

To put it differently, it is important to discern the cause of a storm. Some storms are going to stop because you obey God. Some storms are going to stop out of obedience. If you are a believer, every storm that comes into your life is for your perfection. Even the ones the devil throws at you, they are for your perfection. God will turn it around for your good.

In essence, it is far better to obey God's call than to be thrown into the sea and live for three days in the belly of a great fish. People have told me, "I have the call of God on my life," but never responded to the call to ministry. They acknowledge the call of God, but do not realize that their storm may come because of disobedience, and they will have to confront it.

This is not the message we would want to tell people. We would not want to have to say, *"Throw me into the sea, and it will become calm again. I know that this terrible storm is all my fault"* (Jonah 1:12 NLT).

God's Call & Purpose
For Your Life Never Changes

God's call and purpose for your life will never change. Then the crew said, "Wait a minute, we're going to get this ship safely to shore. We found out that you are not obeying God, but the flesh is going to work through this. We are going to work as hard as we can and we are going to overcome this thing."

You must know that you are not going to overcome the call of God on your life. The scripture says, *"Instead, the sailors rowed even harder to get the ship to the land. But the stormy sea was too violent for them, and they couldn't make it"* (Jonah 1:13 NLT).

We must understand that we are not going to drown it out with noise. We are not going to get too busy that we cannot hear it because the purpose that He ordained for us will never change. The purpose He ordained for your life will never change!

Those on Board in Your Storm
May Plead to God for Their Lives

For that reason, there may be a desperate point in your storm when people around you may cry out to your God. At this point in the storm, the Bible says that the sailors had left their gods. *"Then they cried out to the LORD, Jonah's God. 'O LORD,' they pleaded, 'don't make us die for this man's sin ...'"* (Jonah 1:14a NLT).

In other words, they were saying to Jonah, "We need to identify with something here. Your God is moving amongst us, right now, and He is trying to get something straight. We are not going to pray to our gods because they are not doing anything. We are praying to your God. This is pretty serious when you came on board saying you are running from God and while everything is breaking loose, you're down in the bottom of the ship sleeping. So, we're praying to your God now."

Some People Won't Be Saved
If You Don't Respond to God's Call

If you have that call of God on your life, you need to know that some of the people are falling by the wayside because you are not responding to the Word of the Lord. That is how serious it is! There are people who are ordained to come into the Kingdom not because your Pastor is preaching, but because of the call of God on your life.

Likewise, you may never preach from a pulpit. You may have an opportunity to get with someone in his or her home or at work. Somebody could be born into the Kingdom of God that may have never set foot in a church because he has been around a man or woman of God with a call of God on his or her life like you.

Meanwhile, the sailors were desperate to plead with God to spare their lives. They said, *"And don't hold us responsible for his death ..."* (Jonah 1:14b NLT).

Let me put that another way: "Lord, don't make us responsible for his sin, but we are getting ready to throw Jonah overboard." They rowed hard and tried to save his life, but he was going to have to be thrown overboard.

Finally, he was gone because they realized that God was not going to let them go until somebody obeyed Him. They were recognizing that God was not letting them go and the storm was not moving away until somebody moved into His will, destiny, and purpose.

If You Stand With Integrity & Righteousness, Your Family & Whole Communities Can Be Saved

With this in mind, the storm with your family may not stop until the father moves into God's purpose of integrity and righteousness. Sometimes, fathers do not fully realize that their whole family is off track until they come into the purpose of God.

Until men fully come into their responsibility, whole communities can stay off track. When men move to a place where they are living with full integrity of God, then everywhere they go, they can change a community.

In order to do this, godly men will stand for righteousness on their jobs, and in their businesses and homes because they are men full of integrity. Those with integrity will stand for righteousness. They would rather die than not stand for righteousness and they will change a community. Thank God for godly women who have been standing in the gap, but now it is time for all to find their rightful place in God.

Three Ways to Discern
The Cause of a Storm

Having read about the storm caused from disobedience, I believe that it is essential that we can discern the cause of storms in our lives. The sailors prayed, *"... 'O LORD, you have sent this storm upon him for your own good reasons"* (Jonah 1:14c NLT).

However, not every storm that has come around you is caused from being out of the will of God. You need to discern the storms. Otherwise, you can misinterpret a storm and think that all the things happening around your life is related to you being out of the will of God. There are three types of storms. They are for obedience, for perfecting, and for God's glory. You must discern the type of storm you are going through.

A Storm Can Relate
To Your Obedience

First, God is looking for obedience. A storm can come into your life that relates to obedience. Oftentimes, when you move into a place of obedience, those storms will move away from you because you are moving into the destiny of God.

Jonah had the call and direction of God, but he chose to go the opposite way and said, "Lord, I can't do that." Instead of rejecting God's call, I wonder what could have happened if Jonah had answered his call the first time. One thing about this kind of storm is that when Jonah obeyed, the storm disappeared.

A Storm Can Relate
To Your Perfecting

Secondly, a storm can be for your perfecting. It is to see how you are going to handle the situation and die to yourself, so that God can move you into your God-given destiny. That is a completely different place and level. Usually when you find yourself in those places, no person can help you.

When you obey God, some storms are not going to disappear because they were for your perfecting. Those storms were not moving you into a place of obedience; you were already in obedience.

A storm can surround you and come into your life for your perfecting. Because it relates to your perfecting, that storm can be whirling and whirling and you do not know the time or season on how long it is going to last. It relates to what you are becoming. Those storms were designed for you and they were tailor-made for you. Know that whatever moves me into perfection may not move you into perfection. Your storms for perfecting are tailor made just for you.

When you find yourself in these places, money is not going to get you out. The intercessors are not going to hurry the process because they are interceding and praying. Therefore, God is not about getting you out, but He is concerned about the process.

That is why it is important to discern the storm. Without a question, you have to know that God is not about you coming to church and hearing a good message. God is not about you coming to church and only being encouraged. God is interested in moving you from one place of glory into another place of glory.

Let me explain the importance of this storm. Without any

doubt, God is moving you into a place of being stronger with Him to be more like Him, and even look like Him. At all costs, He is moving you to that place. It is that important!

You may find ourselves dealing with things and saying, "Why am I dealing with this? I'm serving God with all of my heart." Your character will quickly mature through the storm that relates to your perfecting.

Many may think that because they are Christians, they are supposed to be perfect. They may think that nothing is supposed to happen to them, but it only happens with other folk. However, Christians may go through some circumstances that expose pride issues concerning their image and what people think, and many other things.

Sometimes we tell God that we want to be like Jesus. When we tell God we want to be like Jesus, He will begin to expose pride in our lives as He prepares us for great things. He will give opportunities to die to self that Christ would live within us in greater depths. If we want substance in our lives, He is going to give an opportunity to walk through something that is going to expose our true character.

The Lord is going to give us opportunities to walk like Christ. He will give us an opportunity that will expose how we love and handle a situation with love. The opportunity may expose our sin nature, revenge, rebellion, or how we desire to get back at somebody. It may expose what we want to do to people. With ministers, God may not do it behind the scenes, but may do it in front of the people and the nations. He will give us opportunity to walk like Christ and examine our hearts if we are willing to die to self.

We must understand that the Christian life is not a bed of roses, but is a life of being like Christ in all situations. We must never think that our Christian lives are just about coming to church and getting excited about God. He is not going to allow us to carry the substance of His presence without going through challenges.

Your challenges may be different from others, but to keep the substance of God's presence, you will go through something that you think you cannot handle! However, God is with you to become more like Christ and despite the challenge in it, you will have opportunity to be perfected.

When a genuine Christian is going through a trial or test, he must walk through it like Christ. The only thing that matters is that we are going to walk through it like Christ. At the end, after we walk through it, we need to set our goal on hearing Jesus say, "Son or daughter, you did it just like me!"

When things like that starts happening, you will be able to stand before anybody, and see that just you and Christ walked through it and nobody else. Nobody else but Jesus can feel your pain or the depth of your trials, but He is also the only one who can reward you accurately.

He will give us many opportunities to test if we really want to be like Christ and how much we want to know Him. If we have been crying out that we really want to be like Christ, He will give us opportunities that will test if we really want to know Him in the power of His resurrection and the fellowship of His suffering.

You need to recognize the opportunity to show God's love to a person in whatever is happening. With that person, it may be your last chance to look like Christ. It may your last chance to know Jesus Christ in the power of His resurrection and the fellowship of His suffering. He will move you out of religion and into a new relationship with Jesus. Then God can use you to bring His love to others around you and His glory will be seen.

Recognize a Storm
For God's Glory

Thirdly, a storm can be only for God's glory. This means that your suffering is for His glory. When you obey God, you will see the blessings flow in your life. It will be unquestionable that it is God! This is just how God has lined things up for you. God allows some situations and storms to come for Jesus to be glorified.

It is during your greatest storms when the greatest substance and depth is added to your life. At home, you may have a library of Christian books, but none of it comes close to what God does in the process of time when you are going through a storm.

What you experience in the process is more valuable than any head knowledge you attained. *"For our present troubles are small and won't last very long. Yet they produce for us a glory that vastly outweighs them and will last forever! So we don't look at the troubles we can see now; rather, we fix our gaze on things that cannot be seen. For the things we see now will soon be gone, but the things we cannot see will last forever"* (II Corinthians 4:17-18 NLT).

Tell God That You Want
The Reality of His Presence

Therefore, we must walk it out to live in God's presence. Circumstances will show God how we want the reality of His presence in our lives. Let me give a brief testimony of God's presence that manifested in a church youth meeting.

One day, we could not end the service and start the next service. Young people were praying in tongues and standing up giving words. Somebody else stood and gave an interpretation, and at the end of the service, the ministers were on their faces before God. We could not end the meeting. At the back of the church, parents were arriving to pick up the kids and the youth were bringing the parents to the altar. This is an example of what happens when God's presence fills the place. His presence is amazing! Nothing substitutes for that!

In that church service, a man came to that meeting who had been on drugs for about twenty-five years and suddenly, God moved on him. It was a youth meeting; he was not even supposed to be at that service. He was about forty years old and God delivered him powerfully from drugs. I give all the glory to God! Great is our God!

When we tell God that we want the reality of His presence, this is exactly what will happen. When people see believers lying on the floor in God's presence, sometimes, they might think that the believers are crazy. We must realize that is what it takes. The Lord wants to see us stripped, the world wants to see us stripped, and the church needs to see us stripped. Reach out to the Lord. Tell Him how much you want Him. Mean it with all your heart and tell Him that you want the reality of His presence in your life! God hears the heart for intimacy with Him!

If we have disobeyed God's call by getting too busy to hear and obey His plan, the time may come that a sudden storm will arise and shake us. The storm will give us opportunity to obey God's first plan in our lives. Don't wait for that storm to take place. Now is the time to go after God's presence by crying out to Him in prayer and having intimacy in Him.

No matter what happened in the past, I challenge you to go after the presence and glory of God to hear Him. Proceed with God's Word that He first told you to do to fulfill His purpose. Then, you will enjoy God's abundant blessing from reaching people for Christ that others could not have reached!

CHAPTER 2
THE INNER PLACE

"Then the priests carried the Ark of the LORD's Covenant into the inner sanctuary of the Temple—the Most Holy Place—and placed it beneath the wings of the cherubim."

2 Chronicles 5:7 (NLT)

If there is ever a time you need to know how to get in the inner secret place, it is now. In this chapter, I will share how God has designed you to stay in the secret place so you can go after God's presence, and be a carrier of His Glory. His presence with purity, godliness, and Holiness of heart must come first before God, and then He will do great wonders.

As you read this chapter, listen to God's heart to prepare for His Glory to break out because of you staying in the secret place. Learn how to stay in the secret place, so you can have the mind of God, and do His will that brings His peace, safety, order, and protection in your life. In this chapter, I will be sharing specific instruction to prepare fathers, mothers, young people, pastors, and church leadership on how to get in divine order. Then, God's glory can fill the house and change lives.

God's Presence Radiates
From the Inside Out

God designed you to live from the inside out. There is a place inside of us that I call *the inner place.* It is from this place that you are to live and that is what God really desires.

The world lives from the outside in. Constantly, many people are living lives that are influenced by their circumstances, emotions, and things that they go through. Many find that they go down in an attack and up in a mountaintop experience and they are not stable with God's presence and peace. Often times, because we live from the outside, our lives are that way.

However, God made and developed you to live from the inside out. He designed you to live from the inside—*the inner place*, not from the outside. Out of that inner place, you should radiate the presence of God, then you will radiate His presence from the outside. You can feel God's presence in the atmosphere. You can feel it on your body. Some people get chills. When others feel the anointing, they are lying out in the Spirit. His presence radiates from the inside out and in this chapter, my purpose is to challenge you on how to live in this realm of the secret place.

His Glory Breaks Out
Because of Someone's Stay in
The Secret Place With God

When you have been with God in a real way and His presence is on the inside, then that is when His presence is released on the outside. That is how His presence is administered to others. God can do it! Usually, when God moves, somebody has moved to an inner place with God. Generally, when a revival breaks out, most people do not know how it happens, except the person who has been seeking and spending time with God.

Oftentimes, that person does not feel the revival because he is so in there with God that he does not leave his posts. A revived person does not need revival. He does not leave where he is because if he does, it will impact what God is doing. He may understand a revival is going on, but he will stay in this secret place with God. There is a secret place where God has called for each believer to live. I call it *the inner place* and this is what many Christians have avoided.

Many Christians Want God's Blessings, But Don't Want to Be Changed

On one hand, many do not know about the secret place and some just do not care about it. They really do not want God to move into their lives in a real way. They just want to live happy, let God bless them and keep them from problems and situations. They do not come to God in such a way that really changes their lives. They are not looking to be changed. They are just looking for God to make sure they are happy. That is how many Christians live. God exists to make sure they are happy. However, change is what we should want and is the beginning of a new life.

God Moves When Order is in Place

God wants Christians to live from *the inner place.* Everything radiates from that place that you go through in life. You have an inner place. You have a secret place. You have a place that only God should dwell. When God begins to move, there must be order that comes into the lives of people. There must be order into the church, family, and in the community.

Oftentimes, the leaders and the elders, the mature ones, have to begin to get in harmony and in line. Order will first begin with them. For this reason, Solomon summoned the elders of Israel and this is what happened. *"So Solomon finished all his work on the Temple of the LORD. Then he brought all the gifts his father, David, had dedicated—the silver, the gold, and the various articles—and he stored them in the treasuries of the Temple of God. Solomon then summoned to Jerusalem the elders of Israel...* " (II Chronicles 5:1-2 NLT). Solomon was getting the elders in order so God's presence could fill the house.

A Family Prospers When
There's Unity & Divine Order.

To have God's glory fill the house, there has to be a unity of heart and spirit. You cannot be going all over the place or into two directions at once. It is just like a family. They cannot go in different directions for them to prosper and flow. There has to be a unity of heart and spirit. In the scripture, notice that nothing took place until all of the elders of Israel arrived. They could not even move until the elders came into the city. Nothing could take place without them being in order.

Young People Must
Honor Their Godly Parents

For a family to prosper, there must be order, not only with the parents, but also with the young people to honor their godly parents. With young people who have godly parents, peer pressure will tell them to go against some of the things they have been taught, but they need to know why God gave them their godly parents.

Let me share the four main things I tell young people to help them listen to their godly parents and understand God's order. First, I tell them, "When the elders are in line, in other words, when your parents are in line, and follow God in the best way they know how, you can trust their advice and

24

counsel. You can hear your godly parents, even against your friends and other people who are seeping into your life and saying it doesn't have to be that way."

Secondly, I help young people to understand that with other people who never had a godly lifestyle, they will try to influence them against their godly parents. I explain it like this. "There are people who don't have what you have. They don't have the experience you have. They have never been exposed to the things you have been exposed to within yourself. They have never been exposed to living a godly life. They never had it before. When you enter into their lives, all of a sudden, that is something they have never seen before. They may even say to you that it does not have to be that way. That is why it says, in this scripture, that nothing happened until the elders got in line. Above your friends, trust your parents' counsel who have invested their lives in yours."

Thirdly, I explain the importance of their parents. I tell them, "God has put your parents in your life. God handpicked your parents. You might not look at it that way. You might think you could have been born into any family, but God handpicked that you were born into that family. You might say, 'Wait a minute. My parents were a mess.' God still handpicked them."

Lastly, I instruct young people with the two different ways they can mature in a godly family. I conclude with this, "You can grow up in two ways. You can grow up in a godly family and I have seen it both ways. Many people grow up in a godly family, and had everything to lead them in the right direction, and then, they went the wrong way.

Also, I have seen other families that did not have godly advice. When God got hold of them, they became godly for the next generation. They became what they did not even see from their parents. Whether your parents were perfect or the worst in the world, God can still get hold of your life and you can live this way. You can choose to be what they were not. It is incredible! You can impact a whole generation!"

God is Dealing With His Church & Families to Get Into Divine Order

Previously, I shared how young people need to get their lives in order to honor their godly parents. In addition, God is dealing with churches and in correlation with that, He is dealing in the same way with families to get back in order. Order is coming back to the churches that hunger after His presence and they are going to have people that desire order.

Furthermore, people in these hungry churches are going to line up with the Word of God. There are certain things that must get in order. Nothing could transpire until the elders had arrived in Israel. That order is coming back to the church. God is going to raise up some godly people.

To be more specific, God is going to deal with church people that are doing their own things and they will surrender to God's order. Likewise, the same thing is going to take place in a family. If a child chooses to go against a parent that lines up with the Word of God, it will be to his or her own downfall. This thing is that serious!

In other words, children can rebel and take themselves from underneath the covering. They have that power. God provides covering, but a child can choose to come from underneath the covering and decide to walk out and do his own thing. It is the same thing in a church. People can choose to come out from underneath the covering and they can do their own thing.

Therefore, God provides a covering for safety and

protection. The safety is in the covering. The protection is in the covering. God provides parents for this reason. When the child lines up with the parents and is in agreement with them, there is a covering of protection and safety. That should give them liberty to do whatever they need to do, but in the safety of the covering of God.

In comparison to that, the Bible says that the elders had come in and the leaders of the ancestral families of Israel were supposed to bring the Ark of the Lord's Covenant to the Temple from its location in the City of David, also known as Zion.

It says, *"So all the men of Israel assembled before the king at the annual Festival of Shelters, which is held in early autumn. When all the elders of Israel arrived, the Levites picked up the Ark"* (II Chronicles 5:3-4 NLT). Again, here in the scripture, we can read about the order of God. They have people that are trying to pick up the Ark to carry it and they are not in the order of God. The elders have not arrived, but the people are like the young bull that wants to show what it can do. God moves in divine order.

As the family is in order and the child begins to line up with the Word of God for the family, there is safety. It is the same thing in this scripture. When those elders arrived, that is when the Levites moved into position and they were able to pick up that Ark. The scripture says, *"The priests and Levites brought up the Ark along with the special tent ..."* (II Chronicles 5:5 NLT).

Having the Mind of God
& Doing His Will Brings
Peace, Safety, Order & Protection

Divine order brings safety. Before we make a decision,

there is safety when we have God's mind and will. God wants His glorious presence to dwell within us. When all of the elders arrived, the Levites picked up the Ark. We must begin to live our lives from this inner place. We have to live out of that realm. This means that no matter what happens in our lives, we still have to live out of that place.

In other words, our decisions need to come out of that place. Our vision and the mind of God comes out of the inner place. The worst thing that can happen to us is for us to be frazzled. For this reason, we need to desire the mind of God.

In our decisions, it is very important that we have the mind of God. I do not want to be all over the place. I do not want to be wondering, "Can I do it? Should I do it?" No, I want the mind of God and He knows that I want His mind. I say, "Lord, not my mind or will be done, but your mind!" I want the mind of God because in His mind, there is going to be peace, safety, protection, and the order of God and His will is going to be accomplished.

In correlation to that, when the order came, the Levites lifted up that Ark and began to carry it, which represents carrying His glory. God says that there is a signal that people see and hear. God said that when they saw the priests carrying the Ark, it was the signal to the people to move out and get into position.

The scriptures tells it this way, *"Early the next morning Joshua and all the Israelites left Acacia Grove and arrived at the banks of the Jordan River, where they camped before crossing. Three days later the Israelite officers went through the camp, giving these instructions to the people: "When you see the Levitical priests carrying the Ark of the Covenant of the LORD your God, move out from your positions and follow them"* (Joshua 3:1-3 NLT).

28

This is powerful for not only us, but also for young people. It is not just the pastor, the preacher, or leader. But, it includes us. When people see us carrying the presence of God, the Ark of the Covenant, it is a signal for them to follow us. It brings order to their families.

Disorder Brings Confusion & Cannot Change Lives

In contrast to that, if we do not have the mind of God and we do our own thing, it brings disorder and confusion. Actually, disorder in a family comes from a person that says he loves God, but the family does not see him carrying the Ark or obeying God. Disorder brings confusion to their minds because they hear that person say something, but they do not see him carrying the presence of God. If people do not see the priests in line, then they are confused and are misled.

Even as a young person, God has called them to influence people. With the people that God is calling out, the only thing that is going to influence them is when they see him carrying the presence of God.

A minister could be the greatest preacher in the world, but if people do not see him carrying God's presence, then they will not follow that preacher. He can preach and get people stirred up, but it is not going to last, and that message is not going to stay on them and bring transformation.

One can be the greatest teacher or preacher, but if he is not carrying God's presence, people will not be changed. In other words, everybody goes home entertained and feels better, but it does not transform lives unless the life of the vessel being used is truly carrying the Glory of God.

You Will Grow & Prosper In
Things of God When Listening to Someone
Speaking Truth & Carrying God's Presence

A person that is carrying the presence of God can speak and say something and you will grow and abound in the things of God. When the priests are carrying the presence of God, it is not just a great message that you can go home and talk about. Instead, they impart something that goes into your spirit and being. It will enable you to do what you need to accomplish.

In the Bible, we read how God is getting His people in order. They are about to go into the promise land and He is lining things in order. He is starting with the head; he is starting with the elders. He is telling them to cleanse and purify themselves. He is telling them to get themselves ready, and then, get the Ark and pick it up.

When the people see them pick it up, they are going to begin to get in line. They are going to begin to get in order when they see them carrying God's presence. Therefore, there must be evidence that we are carrying the presence of God and this sends a signal to the people. The evidence of God's presence must be the signal that comes out of us. We cannot fake the presence of God. He will not even let us do it. Actually, if we pick up the Ark the wrong way, it means death. That was the reason why Uzziah died. He had touched the Ark, tried to keep it from falling, and he died. We must have God's presence with the right motive to be changed.

Carrying God's Presence
Changes People

In essence, when we carry God's presence, people are changed. To bring change to our city, state, and nation, they need to be impacted by somebody that is carrying the presence of God! We should not only be blessed, encouraged, and have joy with this message, but we need to take it to another level by doing what nobody else has done as it relates to it.

On the other hand, if a minister seeks to entertain, his preaching and teaching is spiritually lifeless because his motive is to entertain people rather than causing them to repent and cry out to God. Entertainment will not change people.

However, change comes when the demonstration of the power of God is present. *"And my message and my preaching were very plain. Rather than using clever and persuasive speeches, I relied only on the power of the Holy Spirit. I did this so you would trust not in human wisdom but in the power of God"* (1 Corinthians 2:4-5 NLT).

A pure heart will not preach or teach with the motive to entertain others, but to bring people to repentance by God's presence.

Purity says, "My preaching is not going to entertain ears; but it's going to bring people to their knees. It is going to bring a greater conviction on their lives. It's not going to bring praise to the entertainer; it is going to bring a conviction for the glory of God that is going to transform lives and move people into their divine purpose."

To carry God's presence—a pure heart is most important! I believe the church is in the condition that it is in because many leaders and the elders have not been carrying the true Ark of the presence of God. I believe that is where it starts. People want to see leaders carrying God's glory and are dissatisfied at attending a church with no power!

People Are Looking For A Leader
With God's True Presence

For this reason, people are looking for someone with God's presence. When a shepherd does not carry God's glory, the people are sitting and they are like sheep without a shepherd. Actually, when the children of Israel were going through the wilderness, if the cloud began to move, that is when they knew it was time to get up and move. They stayed there for weeks until they saw that cloud move.

Model After Jesus &
Carry His Presence

Prepare to get in that inner place with God, model yourself after Jesus, and carry His presence. People run frantically to and fro if they do not see anyone carrying the Ark of the Covenant. At the present, it does not matter what ministry you are attending. Do not model yourself after anyone else right now, but only model yourself after Jesus.

To be in the place with God, you must carry the Ark of the Covenant and this is the number one thing you must do. You need to put this into practice so you will carry God's presence, and it has to radiate because His presence sends out a signal. Then, wherever God wants you to go, you can say that you have never travelled that way before. *"... When you see the Levitical priests carrying the Ark of the Covenant of the LORD your God, move out from your positions and follow them. Since you have never traveled this way before, they will guide you ..."* (Joshua 3:3-4 NLT).

The only reason these people knew what to do is that they saw the priests carrying the Ark. Many people have never travelled this way before. It does not matter how long we have been in church, but where God is taking us, we have never travelled this way before. We are supposed to realize that, "I am meant to travel this way." It does not matter if we have been in ministry for twenty-five years. We should say, "I am looking for God to do something that I have never seen before. I am looking for His hand to move as it has never moved before. I am not looking to model after somebody else."

Therefore, there is no point in duplicating something that has no power. God is about to do something new, something anointed, and something powerful in our lives! God says that we have never travelled this way before. Stop looking around for some model because there are not any. Don't look around and ask yourself which way you should do it.

Moreover, God is saying that the only way you are going to find it is by getting in there with Him. That is when you are picking up that Ark and have decided that you are going to carry the presence of God, no matter what happens. His presence must be more important to you than any other person or thing. To carry His presence, you must be intimate and desperate for Him. Intimacy says, "It does not matter where people are going. It does not matter what direction they are going. I am looking at my life from all angles. I am staying focused on carrying the presence of God. I have never been this way before. Since I have never travelled this way before, God will guide me."

Respect & Honor
God's Presence

I would like to make another point. We must honor and respect God's presence and not be disrespectful to those who carry God's presence. God is saying that when you see the Ark being carried, keep your distance from the ones who are carrying His presence. God says, *"Stay about a half mile behind them, keeping a clear distance between you and the Ark ..."* (Joshua 3:4 NLT).

In other words, God is telling them, "When you see them carry the Ark of the Covenant, a level of reverence and honor moves into your life. You do not just run up on them in any kind of way. When you see someone carrying the Ark of the Covenant of God, you have such an honor for that place. It takes something to carry the Ark of the presence of God, the Ark of the Covenant. It does not matter what an impure vessel does. They cannot fake it. I'm talking about the real power."

In other words, "Don't get so familiar that you don't understand their roles and that they are here to guide you into the place you have not gone before. That distance represents respect. It represents honor. It is not for the priest, but for the presence that they are carrying. That is the only reason why they can carry His presence, because God has done something in their lives and He has given them authority to carry His glory."

Disrespect Occurs If a Child Becomes Too Familiar With His Parents

Children who disrespect their God-given parental authority are those who are in rebellion against God's authority. From the above scripture, God told them to keep their distance between the priests who were carrying God's presence. I would say the same thing about children. They can get so familiar with their parents that they will lose respect for them carrying God's call to watch over their lives.

If a child goes against what the parents have told him, based on the opinion of someone outside the house, it is one of the most troubling and worst things a child can do. God put both natural and spiritual godly parents in our lives. They are there with us through everything.

However, disrespect and rebellion is when the child listens to a strange voice of someone outside of the house who is trying to speak into the inner place. It is rebellion if the child chooses that rather than what God has ordained. That is why God is telling us that we should not get so familiar, even if it is our parents. He is telling the child, "Don't get the attitude and say, 'That's just my mom saying that.' It is like saying, 'That's just God saying that.' God just said that through mom. 'Don't do it son or daughter!'"

Let me illustrate an example of what it means to get too familiar with your parents and not treat their wisdom, instruction, and authority with respect. Today, in this hour, many people in the world are getting tattoos because the world says it is okay. Even in many churches, the young people feel that it is okay. They think the older people missed it. They do not see anything wrong with it. Even though the parents say, "I know the world is doing it, but you don't do it." They say, "Well, this is just a different time from when you grew up." God's Word does not change!

Moreover, a child must never get to the place where he or she is too familiar. As the parents are carrying the Ark of the Covenant of God, the children can see them move out and that is a signal for them because they are about to go to a place they have never been before. I am not just talking about something that is a flesh thing, but I am talking about a more spiritual thing. As a flesh thing, they think that is very smart and it is not a big deal at all. Everything you do will speak of something. What you do on the outside speaks of things that are in the inside.

To see what God says about this, let me refer to the book of Leviticus. *"Do not cut your bodies for the dead, and do not mark your skin with tattoos. I am the Lord"* (Leviticus 19:28 NLT). In other words, it says, *"Don't tattoo your bodies as the world does."* To mark our bodies speaks of defilement. God said that it speaks to Him of our agreement with the world. It speaks to Him that "Now, my children have identified with the world;" it speaks volumes. A person might say, "Why are you making a big deal about that?" It is because the people following you do not have a clear signal anymore. They see that you have a Christian label, but you look like the world and act like the world. They do not know where they are supposed to be going because you look just like the world does. That person is sending the wrong signal to others. You are the model and example for others to follow, not the other way around.

Therefore, they already know where they are, but not where they are going. They know it is more than that. Show them someone that is different. That is who they want to follow. I am just talking about tattoos here, but this carries over in many other areas of life. I am telling you from the heart of God that it speaks volumes.

Let God Put His Name on You
And the World Will Know
You Belong to Jesus

I would rather have God put His name on me, and then the world will know that I belong to Jesus. Some people want to tattoo Jesus on their arms. The Bible says, *"... Obedience is better than sacrifice ..."* (I Samuel 15:22 NLT). As a tattoo, some people want to put Jesus on their skin and say, "I'm honoring Jesus," but this is not honoring Jesus. It is artificial.

Furthermore, God knows how to put His name on you. God can put His name on you and the whole world will know that you belong to Jesus. He will put His name on you—you do not have to put anything artificial on your skin. He will put His name on you and you will live in a place where His name is honored. The world puts tattoos all over their bodies and then, they have to go back, and put a mark over it to cover it up because they are not satisfied with what they once said.

If you already have tattoos, don't feel condemned, but understand what the Word says and move forward in obedience and God's presence.

People have to hear and see a clear signal. That is why we must keep ourselves from the world. In the Bible, God said to purify yourself because He is getting ready to do some great wonders among you. *"Then Joshua told the people, 'Purify yourselves, for tomorrow the LORD will do great wonders among you'"* (Joshua 3:5 NLT).

To put it differently, when you purify yourself, God will display His Holiness through you and display His glory before the world. This is what Moses was explaining to Aaron. *"Then Moses said to Aaron, 'This is what the Lord meant when he said, I will display my holiness through those who come near me. I will display my glory before all the people.' And Aaron was silent"* (Leviticus 10:3 NLT). That is why you keep yourself pure before God. His Holiness and glory will be displayed through you and then, the people will see the evidence of God's presence and will know that He is real.

Purity of Heart Comes First
Before God Does Great Wonders

When you purify your heart, God is getting ready to do great wonders among you. When the people are purified, that is when God begins to do great wonders. If people tried to do this thing religiously and performed all of these things without the purification, God says that no wonders, miracles, or manifestations of His glory are going to happen.

God Will Magnify You Before People If You Stay in That Place To Purify Yourself

For the reason, if you keep yourself pure before God, He will magnify you before others! We do not have to magnify ourselves. We never have to try to make a great name for ourselves. The Lord told Joshua that He was getting ready to make him a leader in the eyes of all of Israel. We never have to lift up ourselves. God will magnify you before the people if you stay in that place to purify yourself, and say, "Lord, it is my greatest desire to carry the Ark of the Covenant." When I call on God, I want Him to show up. When I am praying for somebody, I want the manifestations and the power of God. I want God to be put on display. I am not trying to work up something.

We do not have to be loud when we carry God's presence. However, as you carry God's presence and speak the Word over people, they are going to feel the result of someone carrying the presence of God. The Bible says that as the priests were carrying the presence of God, the water did not move until they touched that water.

In relation to that, we can read it for ourselves in the following scripture. *"'Look, the Ark of the Covenant, which belongs to the Lord of the whole earth, will lead you across the Jordan River! Now choose twelve men from the tribes of Israel, one from each tribe. The priests will carry the Ark of the LORD, the Lord of all the earth. As soon as their feet touch the water, the flow of water will be cut off upstream, and the river will stand up like a wall'"* (Joshua 3:11-13 NLT).

With this miracle in mind, many people say that it only happened back then, but this is what God is doing today! Like this scripture, God is trying to get His people back into living in His presence and power. As you start carrying the real presence of God, and when you start stepping into a situation, order will begin to step into that situation. As you move into a situation and step into it, all of a sudden, order comes to it. When you have intimacy with God in the inner place with purity of heart and you desire living in God's glory and power, this will happen to you. The moment you step into a situation, this is when God's order begins to move suddenly and come into the situation.

In short, this power is available to you. The Bible says that the priests put their feet in the water and the water started dividing. It was so powerful! Great power is released when carrying God's presence! *"It was the harvest season, and the Jordan was overflowing its banks. But as soon as the feet of the priests who were carrying the Ark touched the water at the river's edge, the water above that point began backing up a great distance away at a town called Adam, which is near Zarethan. And the water below that point flowed on to the Dead Sea until the riverbed was dry. Then all the people crossed over near the town of Jericho"* (Joshua 3:15-16 NLT).

Until the priests came in order and carried the Ark, those kinds of supernatural things did not happen for the people. When they stepped into the water, the people were able to walk freely across the dry riverbed. Likewise, there may be many people following you. Do you know how many people are following you because of God's presence that you carry? I am talking about you carrying the presence of God and someone wants to follow you for that reason. That is what we have to be carrying and we can have this by keeping ourselves pure before God.

However, certain things will not happen and there are certain places you cannot go without a sacrifice. They knew this. Before they brought everything together, King Solomon and all of the leaders began sacrificing so many sheep, goats, and cattle and no one could keep count.

In the scripture, it says, *"The priests and Levites brought up the Ark along with the special tent and all the sacred items that had been in it. There, before the Ark, King Solomon and the entire community of Israel sacrificed so many sheep, goats, and cattle that no one could keep count"* (II Chronicles 5:5-6 NLT)!

Without a sacrifice, certain things will not happen and there are certain places we cannot go. This is why it is so powerful to me. The Bible says, *"Then the priests carried the Ark of the LORD's Covenant into the inner sanctuary of the Temple—the Most Holy Place ..."* (Verse 7 NLT). The Ark was outside and they carried it into the inner place. The inner place is that place in you where God is the only one who dwells there.

God's Glory is Not Manifest
With Religious Outward Performance

God's glory will never manifest with religious performance and showmanship. In America and in many countries, many things defile that inner place. In our lives, that is that reason why many things are not happening by God's supernatural power.

It does not matter how educated a person gets. God's presence is not based on the many titles he receives. Nothing can replace God's presence! The only way to come in that place with God is by purifying yourself and coming clean. Get all the mixture out of your life. Then, the temple will become illuminated. When one has intimacy in God, on the inside of him is where he is in the inner place, and that is where the light of the presence of God is deeply illuminated.

In contrast, there are the outside courts of the Holy of Holies. Symbolically, I refer the outer court to religious folk. They are living in the outer court. They know about God, but they will not go into that inner place. They bring their sacrifices. They are going to go to church and do everything they are supposed to do, but they will not enter into the inner place—the Holy place.

In other words, the outer court folk represent the people of God who have no relationship with Him. We can only see something mighty from God when we are in a relationship with Him. They did not have it themselves. That is mostly what we see today. People are very religious, which means they know how to act like people of God, but they do not have that deep relationship. They do not want to go into that inner place. They think the outer court is fine and they are satisfied with it.

Therefore, the inner court represents those who not only know God, but they are also making sacrifices—they are the priests. They know God and even begin to sacrifice some things, but even there in the inner court, the glory is not being revealed.

In other words, we can do all of the right things, but the glory is not being revealed because His glory is only revealed in the Holy of Holies—that is the only place His glory is revealed.

You are the temple of God and God's presence radiates from your inner place—the place where God dwells in you— the Holy of Holies! He shares that place with no one. You must protect and guard your inner place!

God's Glory Manifests
In The Holy Place

I want to emphasize the power of being in the Holy Place. That is where the glory of God will manifest. Even though we have the title as a child of God, He will only reveal His glory in the Holy Place! Herds of people were standing in the outer court, but only a few people were called to minister unto the Lord. Even in the inner court, people are ministering to the Lord, but they are still not letting God into the inner place. They are doing all those right things, but God is not in there. God wants to move from the inside out and this is what I call the inner place—the Holy of Holies.

The Old Testament temple is a symbol of your body being the temple of the Holy Ghost. That old temple spoke of the day we are living right now. In other words, there will be no physical building from inner, outer, and Holy of Holies. Right now, your body is the tent. The inner court is your soul and emotions and is where you are making all your decisions, but they still can be fleshly, even in the inner court.

However, the Holy of Holies is different! That is the only place where God really leads you. He only radiates from that place. Only in that place is He illuminated—the only place that the glory comes out of and flows! The only place is in that Holy of Holies and you must live out of that place. Don't ever let ministry substitute for that. You can get so busy in ministry that you forget to go into the Holy Place. You can get so busy with your calling that you forget to go into the inner place.

Therefore, when you come out of the holy place, ministry just flows everywhere out of us. When being in His presence, ministry can flow out of you—it is incredible! You can sing and singing may not be your gift, but God can still anoint

42

your voice. You may not sound gifted, but when the anointing moves on the people, it impacts their lives. That is amazing! You may not be talented, but He can give you an anointing that will impact and change people's lives. This is a very rare anointing. This is a true anointing!

In relation to this, let me tell you a story about an old man who had a certain anointing. The only thing he did was to come on stage and start dancing. Within minutes, people were flooding the altar and weeping before God. That is all he would do. They said that he was not dancing in front of anyone but God. In other words, the man left the place where he was. He entered into a holy place with God and he started dancing for the Lord. People were just looking, and then the glory of the Lord began to radiate from his dancing because of him being in that place. The people did not even know why they were coming to the altar. They did not know why they were weeping and crying.

What I am saying is that you must not let anyone limit you. Don't let people tell you that you can't do this or that, and you are not gifted in an area. Forget about all of that. Just get into that inner place. You can sing one sentence and the Spirit of God will fall in the place. The anointing will flow in the place. People's lives will be touched because a sound is coming out of that place that tells them that you have been in the Holy of Holies and presence of God.

When people see someone with God's presence, they might say, "I've seen someone carrying the Ark of the Covenant of God." The Holy Place is that place from which you must live and is what you must value most and then you will flow in awesome anointing and power to set others free. Whether you are in leadership, now is the time to make the essential changes in your life to get into God's divine order so that the presence of God's mighty power and glory will manifest through you.

If you are a man, intimacy in God is the most valuable asset that you have in life. This will take you into your godly position and destiny to walk with purity and Holiness, and be a carrier of God's presence as a priest of your home, church, or ministry. If you are a godly woman, make the necessary changes to take time to pray and be a carrier of God's glory. If you are married, start today to intercede for your spouse to become the godly priest of your home.

If you are single, pray for your family, loved ones, and church to have purity and Holiness of heart. As a young person, now is the time to lay down the past. Apply these truths! Go after God's presence! Put Him first place and God will bring you out of every situation where you need deliverance or freedom. He will put His name and stamp of approval on your life.

All things are possible with God as you stay in the secret place with purity of heart and refuse to allow uncleanness in your heart and life. Your *inner place* is where you and God become one in agreement—*"Not your will, but His be done!"*

CHAPTER 3
PURITY OF
HEART

"If you keep yourself pure, you will be a special utensil for honorable use. Your life will be clean, and you will be ready for the Master to use you for every good work. Run from anything that stimulates youthful lusts. Instead, pursue righteous living, faithfulness, love, and peace. Enjoy the companionship of those who call on the Lord with pure hearts."

2 Timothy 2:21 (NLT)

Know a Tree by Its Fruit

When believers keep themselves pure, there will be evidence of the fruit of Christ in their lives. In addition to this, God's approval will come on vessels with purity of heart and wherever they go, the lives of people will be changed. The Bible says that we will know a tree by its fruit.

Purity is Missing
In the Church Today

Therefore, purity is the thing that is missing in the church today. We can sing and have awesome praise services. We have preachers that can preach to us until we are running up and down the aisles, but we do not see much change in the people. We can have great services, but we do not see a transformation of people coming out of sin and into their destiny with God. That means there is some kind of power that is missing. We may be having service after service, but people are not being changed.

Ministers Need to Desperately
Cry Out to God for Change

Today in churches, people can become comfortable coming into church services, sitting in church on Sundays and still living in sin. I really believe that if our churches are not alive, leadership needs to begin crying out to God. I am speaking that as a pastor myself. If my church is not alive, then the leaders, elders, and I have not cried out to God to the place of desperation, so that He will come and change the situation.

It is one thing for the church members to cry out, but it is another thing for the leaders to cry out. It is the same thing in a family. It is one thing for the family as a whole to cry out. It is another thing when the father begins to cry out in his desperate need for the family, and says, "God if you don't change this situation, we will not make it." He must cry and cry until God changes the situation. There is something about the authority of God. People miss it in our churches today, but God moves in order.

The Holy Spirit Flows
Where There is Divine Order

You need to understand when the Holy Spirit is able to manifest God's presence in the midst. Sometimes, people get confused when they see the moving of the Holy Spirit, and they interpret it to mean that anything goes. The Holy Spirit flows in God's order. When there is divine godly order, the Holy Spirit is free to move. When things are out of order, the Holy Spirit is grieved. He cannot flow in disorder. When a family gets in order, the Holy Spirit can move powerfully. Here is the strength of divine order. A mother can be lined up and the kids can even be going for God, but if the father is out of place, they can only go so far because God is a God of order.

Agree With Me for Purity & a Clean Heart
To Rise Up in Husbands & Men of God

"Heavenly Father, we bless you and honor your name. Lord, we thank you, we come before you, and we pierce the darkness with our prayers. In the name of the Lord Jesus, we pray over every man reading this book and for the husband, sons, and family of the woman who is reading this book. We declare the spirit of prayer, the spirit of purity, and the spirit of revival to rise up in this man or woman."

Purity Comes First Before
God Can Do Great Things
Through You, in You & With You

Once you understand that you are priests, one of the things you want to do is to become clean. God said, "I'm not going to move through channels that are not clean. I'm not going to do mighty works in my name, through channels that are not clean."

You Must Be Set Apart Unto God
To Carry God's Presence &
Be Greatly Used by His Power

To carry God's glory, you must be set apart unto God. In the Old Testament, the priests were the only ones that could do the work. They were the ones that had been set apart unto God. As we read that story, it is interesting that twelve of the priests carried the Ark of the Covenant. It is a very powerful story because it says that when they stepped their feet into the water, the water backed up for miles. It backed up a great distance away to a town called Adam.

When carrying God's presence, He will do great things. As soon as their feet touched the water, it backed up. In the Holy Spirit, there is no distance. There are great supernatural and powerful things that God will do through a person or a priest who begins moving into his or her rightful position.

When you begin to know who you are and get into a place to purify and set yourself totally unto God, then it becomes evident that you are carrying the presence of God. When you step into situations and circumstances, they are going to be changed.

If your marriage is not in the place that it should be, it is time to purify yourself. It is not time for your husband or wife; it is time to purify yourself. You are not going to hinder God anymore. This is for real. The church is being purified.

Today, a pure heart before God is the greatest thing you should want. Not having a pure heart is a hindrance to the move of God and the things God wants to do. We must realize that God cannot do things because of impurities in our heart. Preachers can preach without a pure heart and people can be moved because of their gift. However, we must want to move in such a way that our hearts are so pure that God flows through us with no resistance.

God Promotes a Pure Heart
But Demotes Impurity of
Disobedience, Being Out of Order

If we are disobedient and out of order, it will bring us out of God's presence, plan, and will for our lives. King Solomon had just finished dedicating the things that went into the temple, and the first thing he did was call for the elders of Israel to begin to get into position. They were not even the priests. He called for the elders to come and get in position. The Bible says, *"Solomon then summoned to Jerusalem the elders of Israel and all the heads of tribes—the leaders of the ancestral families of Israel. They were to bring the Ark of the LORD's Covenant to the Temple from its location in the City of David, also known as Zion. So all the men of Israel assembled before the king at the annual Festival of Shelters, which is held in early autumn"* (II Chronicles 5:2-3 NLT).

The calling of an elder is serious. Certain things cannot take place until the elders get in position. Sometimes, people are out of order when they try to do something. Prior to Samuel getting there, Saul was out of order when he tried to sacrifice before the Lord. From 1 Samuel 13:7-13, let me tell you how serious that was. Through God, Samuel said to Saul, "God is going to give you victory. Go and wait until I get there, and when I get there, I am going to sacrifice unto the Lord."

Order is essential to have God's presence and walk in His purpose and plan for your life. Saul was a king, but he was not a priest and he could not wait for Samuel to get there. He went and sacrificed by himself. When someone tries to get out of God's order, some powerful things happen. When things are out of order, it stops the hand of God from moving, delivering and doing what needs to happen.

After Saul went ahead and sacrificed, Samuel comes up and says, "What's going on?" Saul says, "I could not wait. I did not know if you would get here in time. I could not wait and the people were impatient. I went ahead and did the sacrifice." Disobedience caused him to be out of order and it cost him the kingdom. Samuel said, "You don't know what you have done. Today, God has taken the kingdom away from you and found another man whose heart is better than yours."

In other words, "God found another man who will follow Him with a pure heart." God found another man with pureness of heart inside of him. The impurity of the heart kept Saul from moving. The next time in I Samuel chapter 15, God told him, "Go in and take over a city and kill everything," but Saul saved some of the animals for himself.

Then, Samuel walks up to the place and says, "What is with all the animals I am hearing? Didn't God tell you to kill all of the animals?" Saul says, "Yes, but we're going to keep these and give sacrifices to God." As a sacrifice to God, he was going to use what God had told him to kill. That is when God says that obedience is better than sacrifice. That day it was over. The Bible says that it was the last day that Samuel saw Saul and he wept all night over Saul. The prophet Samuel had to go and kill the king because Saul would not do it. This is serious with God.

To Have a Pure Heart
Is More Important Than Ministry

God took the kingdom from a man to whom He originally gave it and found somebody with a pure heart. Let me encourage you to prepare your heart before God. Before you get involved in ministry, you need to find purity of heart. In this hour, many people are doing ministry while still living in sin. They are into pornography. They are living with people. They are in sexual sins, they are sleeping with people and then the next night, they are doing ministry, but they are deceived.

Many ministers are so deceived that they do not even realize it. They think the ministry is more important than the purity of heart. The most important thing is to have a pure heart. That is what God honors. You must want a pure heart. It is time for ministers to have a pure heart so they can carry God's presence: *"When all the elders of Israel arrived, the*

50

Levites picked up the Ark" (II Chronicles 5:4 NLT). The Ark represented the presence of God.

To Carry the Presence of God
Will Cost You Consecration &
A Separated Walk

You do not get into a place of purity of God without sacrifice It is going to cost the flesh. If we are not dying to our flesh, we are not going to move with God in His presence. *"The priests and Levites brought up the Ark along with the special tent and all the sacred items that had been in it. There, before the Ark, King Solomon and the entire community of Israel sacrificed so many sheep, goats, and cattle that no one could keep count"* (II Chronicles 5:5-6 NLT)!

At first, the walk with God is not a comfortable walk for some people, but it is a consecrated and separated walk. It costs something to carry the presence of God. It costs something to carry the anointing of God that breaks people through into new dimensions.

It costs something. A death must happen. If one has not experienced any war in his flesh, then he is on the devil's side. That is strong, but it is the truth. If you are crying out because your flesh wants something and you are resisting it, that is when you are in there with God. That is when God is getting ready to put a stamp of approval on your life. That is when He is getting ready to say, "You can carry my presence! You qualify!"

Your flesh may be screaming when warring against sin. Even in your insides, you are warring against it because you want to be so clean. You are crying for the fire to burn. It is time for the fire to burn. In verse 6, the Bible said that the priests had sacrificed so many cattle that no one could keep count! People are not moved when priests call down fire, and there is no fire coming on the people.

Purity & Holiness Begins
At the House of God

It is crucial that you surrender to God to wait in His presence because with purity of heart, you will have the power of God flowing through you. His power will heal, deliver, and save lives that would have been lost if you did not have the presence of God. At times, we need to sacrifice and consecrate ourselves to Him by all night prayer and surrender, such as saying, "God tonight, I'm going in, and I'm just going to wait on you. I am going to pray and call out to you. I don't know what I'm going to do in the next hour or next second, but I'm going to stay in your presence."

To save lives, God can use you as an intercessor. This is the real Christian life. This is the real deal, right here. There are times when your father's life may depend on your prayer life. There may be times when your best friend's life may depend on your prayer life. To move into their destiny, there may be times when your husband or wife may depend on your prayer life. Five or fifteen-minute prayers are not doing it anymore and is not the key to get what God wants to give you. Getting up in the morning and praying while getting into the car is not going to get the move of God that needs to happen. It is going to take your full attention. It is going to take a focus. It is going to take something special to get the move of God. It is going to take real intimacy in God.

To have a great outpouring of glory, it takes purity of heart and you must continually keep yourself pure and ready for His presence to fill you and flow through you. The Bible tells us that all the priests kept themselves pure. Whether or not they were on duty that day, all of the priests purified themselves. It reads, *"Then the priests left the Holy Place. All the priests who were present had purified themselves, whether or not they were on duty that day"* (II Chronicles 5:11 NLT).

You must want your heart pure! You must desire to cry out to Him until there is such purity in you that when others come around you, they feel His manifested presence and want purity of heart. The purity of heart leads to Holiness. Ungodliness holds back the hand of God. If God does not see Holiness, this nation is going to be judged severely. Judgment begins at the house of God, but Holiness should also begin there.

The watchmen or prayer warriors will shout and sing with joy because of seeing the Lord returning to the house of God and a nation. When you are in His presence, He will give you joy. We have joy because we see that the Lord is about to return. The scripture says, *"How beautiful on the mountains are the feet of the messenger who brings good news, the good news of peace and salvation, the news that the God of Israel reigns! The watchmen shout and sing with joy, for before their very eyes they see the LORD returning to Jerusalem"* (Isaiah 52:7-8 NLT).

God's only requirement was for us to purify ourselves. God is going to do it. We just need to purify ourselves. The scripture continues, *"Let the ruins of Jerusalem break into joyful song, for the LORD has comforted his people. He has redeemed Jerusalem. The LORD has demonstrated his holy power before the eyes of all the nations. All the ends of the earth will see the victory of our God. Get out! Get out and leave your captivity, where everything you touch is unclean. Get out of there and purify yourselves, you who carry home the sacred objects of the LORD. You will not leave in a hurry, running for your lives. For the LORD will go ahead of you; yes, the God of Israel will protect you from behind"*

(Isaiah 52:9-11 NLT).

It Takes Sacrifice
To Keep Purity of Heart

To keep purity in your heart, you cannot sell your soul for ungodly entertainment. When you have a pure heart, you will spend time in God's presence. Later on, if you watch movies, you will be convicted of sin and will not watch something that is unclean. That is what it takes to keep purity of heart.

If something is unclean, the pure in heart will immediately stop, pray, and turn off the television. When you are devoted to purity, you will not want uncleanness to invade your spirit. It does not matter if the movie appears to be good or if it is the number one seller. We must keep our hearts pure by not selling our soul for the sake of entertainment. Our hearts are not good ground for anything that defiles or pollutes our spirits.

The unclean entertainment and lusts of the world do not satisfy because God's presence means more to us than anything else. If we watch a movie that is unclean, we will be grieved because we have made the consecration to have nothing to do with it. Therefore, that is the price to have God's presence. We cannot have sin and God's great power in our lives. It grieves the Holy Spirit if we sit and endure curse words, sexual scenes, murders, and those kind of sins to satisfy the pleasure of the entertainment.

The Bible says, *"Thou art of purer eyes than to behold evil, and canst not look on iniquity ..."* (Habakkuk 1:13 KJV). To have God's presence, you must keep your heart focused on purity, and then you will become sensitive to Him. When the Holy Spirit is grieved, you will be grieved. Since the Holy Spirit cannot witness to uncleanness, then I am not going to do it. This is why I am sharing about our need for purity.

There is no way that we can stay pure if we are letting the world feed us with ungodliness and we make excuses by saying it is okay in the name of entertainment. We cannot do it if we cannot keep a pure spirit! This is what it means to live a consecrated life of sacrifice to God. The decision to not watch an unclean movie should be an inward witness from the grieving of the Holy Spirit that says, "That's unclean!"

When we know the Spirit of God, we will discern that it is unclean. To keep purity of heart, you will say, "I'm not going to taint myself. This is what I desire with God. No more curse words or uncleanness can come across the screen or defile my eyes and spirit. Man looks at the outward appearance, but God looks at the heart."

To See God, Maintain a Clean Heart
To Not Defile Yourself

There is a price to have God's presence. After paying money for a movie, if there is something unclean in it, it is better to walk out of that movie. A man with a clean and pure heart will say, "I'm not going to get my spirit defiled. That junk is not coming in me. I'm going to maintain a clean spirit. My goal is set on pleasing my Heavenly Father and He says, 'That's my son right there. He is not going to get himself defiled.'"

The world needs to see clean vessels because when you begin to speak, the mighty presence and power of God will flood out of you and change lives. The Bible says, *"God blesses those whose hearts are pure, for they will see Go*d" (Matthew 5:8 NLT). Some people cannot see God because their hearts are not pure. God blesses those whose hearts are pure for the pure shall see God. To have intimacy with Jesus and His presence in a powerful way to shake our cities and communities for Christ, we must desire a pure heart to honor God in all His ways. The Bible says, *"Teach me your ways, O LORD, that I may live according to your truth! Grant me purity of heart, so that I may honor you. With all my heart I will praise you, O Lord my God. I will give glory to your name forever"* (Psalms 86:11-12 NLT).

Your number one desire should be, "Lord, grant me purity of heart." The scripture relates the Holy Spirit to having purity of your heart. It says, *"But you desire honesty from the womb, teaching me wisdom even there. Purify me from my sins, and I will be clean. Wash me, and I will be whiter than snow. Oh, give me back my joy again. You have broken me—now let me rejoice. Don't keep looking at my sins. Remove the stain of my guilt. Create in me a clean heart, O God. Renew a loyal spirit within me. Do not banish me from your presence, and don't take your Holy Spirit from me"* (Psalms 51:6-11 NLT).

Purity Does Not
Mix With Sin

To have purity, there is a price to train yourself to not be defiled by sin, and spend time to sacrifice and consecrate yourself to Him in prayer. You have to discipline yourself to hear the Word of the Lord and wait in His presence. The word *"purity"* can be defined as "freedom from mixture." We must get the mixture out of our lives. God cannot move if we have been defiled. God cannot move at the level He wants to move. Purity is freedom from mixture and corrupting elements. That is purity. It is cleanness or clearness. When a heart is pure, it is clean and there is clearness of desire.

The Bible says that all things are pure to those whose heart are pure (Titus 1:15). When your heart is pure, there is cleanness about it and you see with cleanness. You do not see the defiled things, you do not see lust and you are not desiring it. You are not chasing after all those crazy things because there is a pureness about your heart. Therefore, you cannot see it because your heart is pure.

When your heart is pure, you are attracted to pure and godly things, and these eternal things feed your spirit. To "purify" means to get rid of impurities or pollution and to free from incorrect or corrupting elements. Purity means you are freeing yourself from corrupt and incorrect things.

The word "pure" means that it is perfect, unmixed, cleansed, and clear, it is free from anything that taints, impairs, or infects and free from defects.[1] When God sees a pure heart, He sees a perfect heart, even though you know you are not perfect. You must want a pure heart because you know what God is about to do, and He can only do it through a pure heart! You are being perfected for the greatness and glory of God.

A pure heart is faultless. In other words, God cannot find fault in your heart. It is blameless and pure. God cannot find blame. It is free from sin or guilt. Another definition of pure also means "virgin."[2] The world teaches our young children, girls, and boys to lose their virginities as fast as they can. However, they do not understand that it represents their purity. They can give it away freely and they do not even know they have just been made impure. The world says that it is attractive, but God says that when He created a virgin, He purposed for one to be pure until he or she is married.

Relating to purity of heart, I will give you seven scriptures and I will show you the importance of purity in your life. First, the Bible says you were cleansed from your sins when you obeyed the truth. Obeying the truth is one way to be cleansed. *"You were cleansed from your sins when you obeyed the truth, so now you must show sincere love to each other as brothers and sisters. Love each other deeply with all your heart"* (1 Peter 1:22 NLT).

Secondly, when you expect to see Christ as He is, you will keep yourself pure as Christ is pure. The Bible says, *"Dear friends, we are already God's children, but he has not yet shown us what we will be like when Christ appears. But we do know that we will be like him, for we will see him as he really is. And all who have this eager expectation will keep themselves pure, just as he is pure"* (1 John 3:2 NLT).

Thirdly, it is crucial that you keep yourself pure before God so that you can be used as a clean vessel for His honor. You do this by pursuing righteous living, faithfulness, love, and peace. We read this as follows: *"If you keep yourself pure, you will be a special utensil for honorable use. Your life will be clean, and you will be ready for the Master to use you for every good work. Run from anything that stimulates youthful lusts. Instead, pursue righteous living, faithfulness, love, and peace. Enjoy the companionship of those who call on the Lord with pure hearts"* (II Timothy 2:21 NLT).

Fourthly, God tells us to not share in the sins of others and keep ourselves pure. This is what it means to have purity of heart. The Bible says it this way: *"Never be in a hurry about appointing a church leader. Do not share in the sins of others. Keep yourself pure"* (1 Timothy 5:22 NLT).

Fifthly, we are the bride of Christ. To be ready for Him, we must keep ourselves pure to give Him our undivided devotion and attention. We must consecrate all of ourselves to be loyal to Jesus as our husband. The scripture says, *"For I am jealous for you with the jealousy of God himself. I promised you as a pure bride to one husband—Christ. But I fear that somehow your pure and undivided devotion to Christ will be corrupted, just as Eve was deceived by the cunning ways of the serpent"* (II Corinthians 11:2-3 NLT).

Sixthly, when we are Christians, we are sincere to give up all sin and we allow no corruption to defile our hearts. We do this by having nothing to do with impurity, sexual immorality, and lustful pleasures. The Bible says, *"... And I will be grieved because many of you have not given up your old sins. You have not repented of your impurity, sexual immorality, and eagerness for lustful pleasure"* (II Corinthians 12:21 NLT).

Lastly, the Bible says that the first thing they needed to do was to purify themselves and then, they had the ability to purify others. It reads, *"The priests and Levites first purified themselves; then they purified the people, the gates, and the wall"* (Nehemiah 12:30 NLT).

The Glory Will Fill Your Temple
When There is Purity of Heart

When your heart is pure with your total attention on the Lord, you will worship God with all your heart and really mean it. The Bible tells us that there was something that happened after they were purified. It says, *"Then the priests left the Holy Place. All the priests who were present had purified themselves, whether or not they were on duty that day. And the Levites who were musicians—Asaph, Heman, Jeduthun, and all their sons and brothers—were dressed in fine linen robes and stood at the east side of the altar playing cymbals, lyres, and harps. They were joined by 120 priests who were playing trumpets"* (II Chronicles 5:11-12 NLT).

The Levites, musicians, and all their sons and brothers were dressed in fine linen, which represents righteousness. The 120 priests joined with them as they were playing trumpets. It is interesting that there were 120. This relates to the day of Pentecost with the 120 in the upper room.

God honors purity of heart. The glory filled the temple after the trumpeters and singers were in unison to praise and give thanks to God, saying, "He is good. His faithful love endures forever!" We read this as follows: *"The trumpeters and singers performed together in unison to praise and give thanks to the LORD. Accompanied by trumpets, cymbals, and other instruments, they raised their voices and praised the LORD with these words: 'He is good! His faithful love endures forever!' At that moment a thick cloud filled the Temple of the LORD. The priests could not continue their service because of the cloud, for the glorious presence of the LORD filled the Temple of God"* (II Chronicles 5:13 NLT).

There is no substitute for the glory. You cannot fake it. You cannot put it on. You cannot conjure it up. It is purity of heart. At that moment, a thick cloud filled the temple of the Lord and the priests could not continue their service because the cloud of the glorious presence of the Lord had filled the temple. God cannot fill unclean temples with His glory. He fills clean vessels with the glory.

Take time alone to pray and open up your heart so He can fill your temple with His glory and you can carry His presence wherever you go. Do this by surrender. Ask Him, "God, what sacrifice do you want from me?" Then, be willing to obey what He tells you. The other thing to say is "Lord, take me to a new place of surrender. Purify my heart, oh God."

If you are not saved today, do not deceive yourself. You know you are not saved, and need to come back to Jesus and consecrate everything to Him. If you did not surrender when you once said the sinner's prayer, and if you are not sure that you are going to Heaven, you can be sure today. Surrender your life to Jesus, and not by repeating words. The devil can repeat words and he will never be saved.

In conclusion, a surrendered life to Jesus is what saves a person! If you never felt salvation in a real way, even if you have been in church all of your life, this is the day to surrender to Him. Just yield your heart to Jesus and surrender all to Him today.

CHAPTER 4
BAPTISM OF PURITY

"Then Joshua told the people, 'Purify yourselves, for tomorrow the LORD will do great wonders among you.'"

Joshua 3:5 (NLT)

If there is ever a time when laymen and ministers need the baptism of purity so they can have God's glory and power, it is now! In chapter 2, I shared the scriptures and teaching on Joshua chapter 3 and related it to the inner place. In this chapter, I will review these scriptures again, relate it to laymen and leaders, and focus on the *baptism of purity*.

God is calling His church for a fresh *baptism of purity*. Understand why many leaders preach God's word with no demonstration of power and people are not changed. Many need to get rid of the defilement and be pure vessels before God. We must know the reason why God's mighty power can only move through clean vessels that have a *baptism of* purity and reverence for His presence. If you have been struggling and trying to carry your ministry, now is the time for change.

If you have not been able to see and carry God's presence, learn what you must do to get rid of the idols that stand before you and how to have Holiness of heart. If you want people to follow you, they must see God's presence in you and flowing out of you. It is God's heart for ministers to have a *baptism of purity*. For this reason, God instructed ministers to carry His glory and then, great power will manifest in their lives and ministries with evidence that God is real.

God Moves Through
Clean Vessels

The reason that some churches are at a standstill is that the priests are not carrying the presence of God because they are not clean vessels. The priests are not carrying the Ark of the Covenant as they should, and many have defiled themselves. Often, the world mocks the church.

Many of the ministers are caught up in their own ministries and building their ministries, but God did not call them to build their ministries. God called them to carry the presence of God. He can only move through clean vessels that have the *baptism of purity* and like never before in history, they will cross over into realms of the supernatural glory of God.

Right now, you may be like Joshua and all the Israelites who arrived at the banks of a river, and camped in front of it. The river does not look like it is going to part before you but there is going to be power that parts that river (Joshua 3:1 NLT).

Before pastors, ministers, and leaders can cross that mighty river by carrying God's glory, they must have the *baptism of purity*!

The signal for the people to move was when the priests were carrying the Ark of the Covenant. They stood before that river and it was a mighty river, and they could not cross it. There was a signal and it was, *"When you see the priests carrying the Ark of the Covenant, get in position and follow them"* (Joshua 3:2-3 NLT).

God Didn't Call Ministers
To Carry a Ministry,
But to Carry His Presence

He never called ministers to build a ministry. He called them to carry His presence and glory. When the people see the presence of God—the glory of God, they know to move into position. They will know that they are getting ready to cross the river. They know that they are getting ready to get into the promise that God has ordained for them. When they see the real presence on their lives, they know their rivers are beginning to part.

They know that the promise land is about to be entered into. They know that everything God promised is going to happen. The priests are carrying the signal. The priests have to carry the presence of God or the people do not know the next move or the next step to take (Joshua 3:3 NLT).

Some have been staying in the same place. God says that when you see the priests carrying the presence, do not stay in the same place. It is time to move out. For a long time, some have been going around the same mountain, but God has put somebody in your midst or people in your path that are carrying the presence. God says to get in position. You are getting ready to move into position because God is going to show you how get to the place of carrying the presence. This is very important!

A pastor or man of God is not the only priest who is called to carry God's presence. When you read Revelation chapters 1 and 2, the Bible clearly states that the people of God are kings and priests to their God. That means when people see you carrying the presence of God, the Ark of the Covenant of God, then the people around you are going to begin to get in position. People around you are going to begin to line up. The presence on you will lead them into the will of

God, the ways of God, the promises of God, and the presence of God.

People Can't See God's Presence
Because of Idols Standing Before Them

If the priests are not carrying the presence, they cannot guide them into the destiny that God has ordained for them. This is the day of the *baptism of purity*. This is where priests now have to move out of this place. Many leaders have become an idol to the people. The people cannot see the presence of God because the idol is standing before them. This is the real deal. God is awakening His church and people! It is a great day and a great place to surrender. We must have another level of yieldedness. Right now, cleansing and purification must happen in our lives.

See God's Glory Before You

As you carry God's glory, Zoe life is on the inside of you—in your inner most being. Don't count on your past experiences anymore. Just see the glory of God before you. When you see the presence of God, it is the signal to move out. That is the signal that God is getting ready to do some miracles for you. Therefore, you must know how you get the presence. *"Then Moses said, 'If you don't personally go with us, don't make us leave this place. How will anyone know that you look favorably on me—on me and on your people—if you don't go with us? For your presence among us sets your people and me apart from all other people on the earth'"* (Exodus 33:15-16 NLT).

In other words, Moses is saying that "the only difference between him and everyone else on the face of the earth is your presence. That is the only difference between me and your people and everyone else on the face of the earth." We should pursue His presence more than any other thing because that is the distinguishing factor between us and everyone else. That presence does not just come because we have a Christian title.

We Cannot Fake God's Glory

We cannot fake the glory. There is no substitute for the glory! There is no counterfeit for it; nothing looks like it. Moses recognized something and said, "God, there are some great things that are getting ready to happen, but I'm not going to leave this place unless your presence goes with us." Some of us must be that same way in prayer.

We want to get deliverance by someone laying hands on us, but if we enter into a place of consecration and really give ourselves to God, we can be delivered while fasting. This tells God that we are serious. Faith without works is dead. We can have faith all day long, but until God sees some work, nothing is going to happen. He has to see some manifestation of our faith. "Show me your faith," James said, "and I'll show you my works." It's not enough to just believe God. He said that He was going to demonstrate something.

James says it this way. Faith is made perfect by works. Perfect faith is demonstrated by works (James 2:22). This shows God that I really believe Him when I do what He says. When I do what He says, that work demonstrates my faith to God.

Purity is the Missing Link

God will do great things when we are baptized with purity. This is what Joshua tells the people. *"Then Joshua told the people, 'Purify yourselves, for tomorrow the LORD will do great wonders among you'"* (Joshua 3:5 NLT). That is powerful! Right now, that is the missing part in the church. It is the purification. Defiled vessels are trying to do the work of God. Defiled vessels are trying to bring forth a pure praise. Defiled leaders are trying to bring forth a penetrating word from God. It can only come out of Godly vessels. Leaders must be headed to this place of purity. Many struggles are happening in people's lives and this relates to the fact that there is too much mixture in their lives.

Things are usually most effective when they are pure. When something is pure, it is almost too strong. You have to dilute it down. I am talking about its pure state. In the book of Revelation, when God talks about Heaven, it is amazing how many things He says that are pure. The gold is pure gold; the river is a pure river. That means it is undefiled. There is nothing but cleanness in it. The Bible says that God's eyes are too pure to behold evil.

God said, *"To the pure I will show myself pure"* (Proverbs 18:26). We cannot see Him if we are defiled. He says, "To the pure in heart, they shall see God" (Matthew 5:8). He says that if we do not get our hearts pure, we cannot see God. We cannot see Him as we want to see Him. Inside of us, God wants us to have this desire of such purity that we will not get satisfied unless we are moving into that place of purity.

Repentance Is
The First Step to Holiness

The Bible says that we have not warred against sin unto death, looking to Jesus, the author and the finisher of our faith (Hebrews chapters 11-12). This is a strong Word. In other words, He has encouraged us that we have not come to the place where we war against sin, even to the death.

68

The vessels being cleansed are saying, "I am going to see with pure eyes. I am going to be a channel for the pureness of God." It is pureness and then its holiness. Without holiness, no man shall see God (Hebrews 2:14). The first place is repentance, but that is not the ending place. That is the first step to holiness. Genuine Godly repentance is the first steps towards purity and holiness. There is no age group to it. Someone could be twelve years old and have a pure heart and pure spirit and God's glory can flow through that vessel.

People Won't Follow You
If They Don't See God's Presence
In and Through You

If people cannot see God's presence in and through you, they will not follow you. Through Joshua, God told the people, purify yourselves, then lift up the Ark of the Covenant.

His Word gives great faith and strength in knowing that you can purify your heart to the degree that you have the manifestation of the power of God that is going to flow the entire time. The power cannot help but flow when you are a pure vessel. You must want it! Right now, you must be done with religion and tired of it!

You must hunger for the real manifestation of the power of God. The river has to part. *"In the morning Joshua said to the priests, 'Lift up the Ark of the Covenant and lead the people across the river'"* (Joshua 3:6 NLT). I want to emphasize it again. Lift up the Ark because if the people do not see the presence, they are not going to follow. He said, "When you get the presence, lead the people." If we do not lead them, then we will not be able to bring them into God's presence. If we carry the presence, lead them across that river. In other words, we are showing them how to walk. We are showing them how to move into what God has called them to be. We lead them. We do not have to command them; just lead them.

Train the People to Follow
God's Presence & They Will Know
If God is With You

In the Old Testament, God trained His people to follow His presence. The Bibles says that it was a cloud by day and a pillar of fire by night. He trained them to follow His presence. The people camped when the cloud—the presence of God, had stopped. They stayed until the cloud moved. If that cloud stayed for three weeks, they stayed three weeks. When that cloud began to move, they jumped from that place. They began packing because they were not going to separate themselves from His presence. He trained them not to follow a man, but only His presence. A man will die, but the presence will go on and God will lay His presence on someone else to lead the people.

As a leader, your requirement is to go ahead of them. You cannot tell people to pray if you are not praying. You cannot tell them to fast if you are not fasting. You must go ahead of the people. That is the signal to the people. God put a leader around you to show you the way that you ought to go. If you see the presence of God, you need to follow your leader. He or she is leading you by his or her walk. Your pastors will teach you by their walk. *"The LORD told Joshua, 'Today I will begin to make you a great leader in the eyes of all the Israelites ...'"* (Joshua 3:7 NLT).

You do not have to make yourself a great leader. God says, "I will make you a great leader amongst the people." You never have to make yourself a great leader. If you go in there with God, you cannot help but to become a great leader. God is the only one that can magnify you as a great leader.

70

The way He does it, nobody can stop it. God will jump over people who went before you and put you in that position.

God Trains in the Holy Ghost
Through Obedience

God is giving commands to obey. By disobedience, many men and women of God miss being trained by God. Obedience is how God trains us in the Holy Ghost. The Holy Spirit is always speaking to us if we are children of God. If we find ourselves arguing with God, challenging Him, or going back and forth with Him, we are going around a mountain. When God speaks to you, obey—that is the only thing that you have to do—that is the training.

There were levels that God took Moses in obedience. The first time the children of Israel complained, God said, "Moses, strike the rock and water will come out." Moses struck the rock and water came out. The next time he did it, He said, "Speak to the rock" (Numbers 20:8). In anger, Moses struck the rock and water gushes out (Numbers 20:11).

This is the point that I am making. Moses was being promoted by following God. In other words, He was taking him from a place of striking the rock to just speaking to it. God was taking him higher in levels. In his anger, he struck the rock and because he did it, God said, "Moses, this day you shall not enter the promise land." It was not because he struck the rock. It is because God said, "You didn't give me the glory." He did not enter into the promise land because he was not obedient to give God the glory.

In other words, God was saying, "If you had done what I said, I could have had glory out of it, but you did it your way. In this case, I could not get glory out of it due to the people thinking that because you hit the rock, water came out. I wanted to show them that all you had to do was speak to it and water was coming forth." God was taking him up and said, "If you had done it that way, glory would have come to my name." If people had seen it, they would have said, "Glory to God!" Moses took the glory by his disobedience. Obedience is so important. If you do not obey the specific instructions that He told you, God will not get any glory.

Let God's Presence Lead You

When a man is serious about God's Glory, the Lord is serious about purification. There is a direct correlation between miracles and wonders being performed around you. Purification is the prerequisite for God to do some great things. Holiness is what holds back the judgment of God.

The presence of God is what leads you. In the book of Joshua, the Ark of the Covenant led the Israelites across the Jordan River. *"So Joshua told the Israelites, "Come and listen to what the LORD your God says. Today you will know that the living God is among you. He will surely drive out the Canaanites, Hittites, Hivites, Perizzites, Girgashites, Amorites, and Jebusites ahead of you. Look, the Ark of the Covenant, which belongs to the Lord of the whole earth, will lead you across the Jordan River"* (Joshua 3:9-11 NLT)!

Finally, when they came to the other side, God said to Joshua, "Command the people to pick up rocks from the floor of the river, so it will be a memorial to them of what I did for them." In other words, they never saw the bottom of that river. They picked up the rocks. God said, *"Take those twelve stones and put them in a pile so when your children come to you later and say, Dad, what are those stones for? Those stones represent the rocks that we gathered from the bottom of that river on dry ground. It is when your God separated the waters for His people."*

72

When He ends it, He says, "When the last person finally steps over, tell the priests to step out of the water." As soon as they stepped out of the water, the water came rushing back. God's heart is that you as a believer, pastor, or minister will be *baptized with purity* by keeping clean before God. As you take time to develop intimacy with Jesus as first in your life, you will see God's great miracles manifest through you!

CHAPTER 5
YIELDEDNESS
TO GOD

*"... God opposes the proud but favors the humble. So humble
yourselves before God. Resist the devil and He will flee from
you. Come close to God, and God will come close to you ...
Humble yourself before the Lord, and He will lift you up in
honor."*

James 4:6-10 (NLT)

It is crucial that you understand what it means to yield to
God. Among other things, in this chapter, I will illustrate
how fathers yield to the Lord by setting a godly model for
their children and family to follow. I also want to encourage
men the joy of *Yieldedness to God*, how it shows character
when leading by example, and how it affects their children
and the entire home to follow in their footsteps. Understand
why your children need to see their dad crying out to God
and being yielded to God.

Next, I want to show how to keep a right heart, watch
your words, and not let negative words grip you and take you
out of God's peace. Then, understand how to yield to God to
let Him take hold of you, so He can carry you in His presence
and cause you to see things in the spirit as He sees them
according to His Word.

Understand how *Yieldedness To God* produces action.
Start yielding your heart in a fresh way to God. The more
you yield, the greater God uses you. After that, I will show
you how God will test you for tenderness and yieldedness
before He gives you an assignment to use you mightily.

Lastly, understand how to yield to God by praying with expectation, putting value on it, and releasing miracles to happen.

Set a Godly Model
For Others to Follow

It is better that you yield to God rather than doing your own thing. It is better to be obedient than being comfortable. There is a blessing when yielding to the Holy Spirit. You must be conscious that everything you do sets an example to others. Jesus modeled out the Kingdom of God by how He lived. Everything you are doing should be the model for other people to follow.

In this chapter, I will focus on encouraging men and women. In particular, I will share how to yield to God, be a godly model for your children and others to follow, and be the leader God has called you to be. Thank God for the women who have carried their families through challenging times. Now is the time for men to become true men of God by taking their God-given place to lead their families into new levels of purpose and destiny.

God has built leadership inside men and women and everything they do sets an example. It is one thing for a woman to lead the household, but it is another thing for a man to lead the household. Men are important!

God has set the order of the authority of a father and mother in the home. Fathers, you can greatly impact your children to follow you. God has ordained fathers to be the head of the home and has given them authority to set things in order. *"For a husband is the head of his wife as Christ is the head of the church ... Husbands love your wives just as Christ loved the church and gave his life for her ..."* (Ephesians 5:23-30 NLT).

Adam had the authority to kick the devil out of the Garden of Eden when he tempted his wife Eve. Today, the father has the authority and provides the covering to kick the devil out of his family.

Children know the voice of their father. It is amazing that even animals know the voice of authority. In households, sometimes a wife will say something three times to the children before they move and the dad will just have to look in the direction of the child. He does not even have to speak. If he has to speak, it brings a higher level of correction. I do not mean it in a dominating way; God put a level of authority in a man and that is why it is important for men to be in place.

For this reason, it is important for men to lead the way that God ordained and to be there to make sure the family is covered and is in line with the will of God. Often, it has been the women carrying that responsibility.

To be in place, it speaks volumes for men. That is why it is important for men to be visible in the homes, in the communities, and on the job. It is impossible to lead from the rear. We have to lead from a visible place. We have to be seen. God is looking to use godly men who will take their ground, be visible, and be the example. Lead in prayer, lead in worship, lead during challenges, lead in love, and lead by example.

That is why there is a demonic attack set against fathers and the family. The devil sees something in the spirit of men that if they rise up and truly walk in their God-given authority and begin to clearly see, they will see what God has put inside of them, and it is over for the devil. We men must have this attitude, "If nobody else shows up, I will show up. Just by the fact that I am visible, speaks volumes. Just the fact that I am here, speaks volumes that are louder than words. Devil, the buck stops here." As a man walks yielded to God, He has all authority to cover his family under God's authority.

A child feels secure when they know that dad is in the house. Many children have been afraid at night because dad was not there in the house. Because dad is not home, a fear comes on them when they are in bed and they are afraid of what could possibly happen to them. There are generations of children growing up in fear and they do not even understand the fear they have because they do not have a dad and the sense of security and safety.

Therefore, when a godly dad is in the house, it brings the sense of security and safety to the family. I am not referring to abusive dads but those who walk in righteousness. There are too many men missing in action but God shall turn that around, beginning with us. Fathers, we are models; we are examples. Men who go to church need to encourage the ones that do not attend church. Don't just let the pastors and elders do it. Say to them, "Brother, we missed you. We need you to show up. We need you in place."

Children Need to See Their Dad
Crying Out to God

In the church and in everything, men need to be visible. Children and our families do not only need to see the strength of the man, but they need to see the tenderness of the man. If your family never sees you weak before God, they may never learn how to depend upon God for themselves.

If you are too strong of a man that you can never cry out to God, ask Him to touch you. Your children need to see you cry out to God. They need to see you on your face as you are pouring out your soul to the Lord. *"O my people, trust in him at all times. Pour out your heart to him, for God is our refuge"* (Psalms 62:8 NLT).

Your children need to see you lying out before God. They need to see your example. That is very important for they will not only see your strength, but they will see you being tender, sensitive, pliable, and yielded to God and this sets an example for your children to yield to God.

It tells them that their dad needs God. They are going to face things in life where they are going to need God. If you never showed them how to get hold of God, they are going to come across some things that they are going to need God in a very desperate way.

Men Demonstrate Character
When They Lead by Example

When a man leads by example, he is displaying his character. If no other church or organization will show strong men, then our churches need to have that. Sometimes, men may miss it, but when we do, we need to repent, and get back in place. We need to cry out for our brothers and for ourselves. In Psalms chapter 51, there is something about repentance when David began to cry out to God. He said, "Lord, I have sinned against you. I have rebelled against you." Then he says, "Cleanse me, oh God. Cleanse my heart. Cleanse and purify my heart, oh God."

In verse 11, David was going after purifying his heart and he told God, "Take not your presence from me." That was a valuable thing that he had. He continues to say, "… so that I can show sinners your ways." The power of cleansing goes beyond saying that you are sorry. When you truly repent, you change and your life turns into a changed lifestyle. In the above scripture, David was taking on a spirit of change that was about to come. In his repentance, David did not just say that he was sorry, but a purifying and cleansing repentance enabled him to take on God's nature. In that repentance, a godly spirit began to be released on him.

In other words, you are not just saying you are sorry, but your heart and life is changed. Repentance says, "God, I'm saying that I'm sorry because I need to be purified and I'm about to show sinners your ways." Repentance is not just saying, "I'm sorry, Lord" but there is a part to repentance that means, "I'm going to show you God that I repented by the turning from my ways!"

God is saying, "Come forth—business leaders, men of God, come forth—husbands and fathers in our communities, great examples, come forth!" We need a prayer like that over our nation.

Don't Let Negative Words Grip You & Take You Out of God's Peace

If people speak negative words to discourage you, it is the plan of the devil to move you out of God's peace. Get back in His presence and do not let it distract you. When you have been praying, waiting upon God, and cultivating the presence of God, people may make a judgment of you and become critical. I want to encourage you because the devil is very subtle.

What a person says can get you off-track. On the inside, it can cause you to be discouraged. To avoid discouragement, grow more intimate in the heart of God by being in prayer and in His word. Worship Jesus—rise above all the reasoning and words of people. You have to know your place in Christ because carnal people will judge you by the outward things, look at your flesh, and say things they do not know or understand. Keep yourself bathed in the presence of God and give yourself over to Him. Everything that you do should be anointed and that should be your expectation!

All of the words and spirit that pours out of you should be anointed. That is the expectation you should have. That is not arrogance or pride when doing the right things as you are going after God. If you are not doing the right things, then it is different. While you give yourself over to God, it is not boastful when it is the truth. You have to rise above words and see that your goal is to be like God and express His love and life in the earth.

Every revival has had tremendous emotionalism going in it; but at the same time, the presence of God was moving powerfully. With every revival in history, there were great emotional things going on in the midst of it. When God gets hold of you, your emotions, flesh, and spirit are going to be affected.

Settle it in your heart that if people speak to you a negative word, you will not let that word get you off course. When you will not let negative words affect you, all of a sudden, you will be in a place with God that you have not been. God will be holding you in that place as He takes you higher in His wisdom and understanding and in His presence.

Refuse to be moved by negative words. Be moved by God's Word and Spirit. Someone can speak to you a negative word and you can be off track because of what was said. It is very important that you never let people discourage you because of the words they say. You are not what people say you are. God has already defined you and you are what He says about you, created in His likeness and image—fearfully and wonderfully made.

If you are in leadership or moving into it, you are going to get negative letters and e-mails. Some people will tell you what they do not like about you, what you said or did. Others will say that they do not like your advice. You are going to get it and if you do not know who you are in God, you are going to be messed up. Stand in the peace of God and keep your focus on Jesus.

Stay in agreement with God's Word and tell yourself, "I'm going after God's presence. That negative word or attitude is not going to bother me. I'm not trying to convince someone of anything. I am not trying to impress that person in any way. I want to be genuine before God and He loves a genuine heart. I was created not to please man, but to please God in all I do.

When God Takes Hold of You, He Will Carry You Away in His Presence & Cause You to See Things in The Spirit

You must yield to the Holy Spirit and let God take hold of you and He will carry you away in His presence. Before Ezekiel saw anything and before God revealed anything to him, God had to take hold of him. The scripture says, *"The LORD took hold of me, and I was carried away by the Spirit of the LORD to a valley filled with bones"* (Ezekiel 37:1 NLT). Therefore, before his next assignment was given, and before he could see the dry bones, God had to take hold of him and that was the first thing that had to happen. If that had not happened, he would not have seen a thing. You will see more, and more will be revealed to you as you grow in greater intimacy with God.

The Spirit of the Lord took hold of him and he was carried away. The Spirit of the Lord took him away to the valley filled with bones. He was looking at all the bones across the valley. I want to emphasize that if God had not taken hold of him, he would not have seen the dry bones.

82

That is so critical because God wants our eyes to see certain things.

In other words, if we do not allow God to take hold of us, there will be things we will not be able to see accurately and clearly for our families, our children, and our futures. We will not see the next assignment or direction as it relates to jobs and all those kinds of things.

The most important thing is that you need to allow God to take hold of your life. You need to admit that you do not know the way, but God knows and yieldedness is most important!

Faith Relates to Yieldedness
That Produces Action

Often, we say that faith is believing. *"Faith is the substance of things hoped for and the evidence of things not seen"* (Hebrews 11:1 KJV). Without faith, it is impossible to please God. All things are possible to him that believes. Without faith, it is impossible to please God, but somehow we have associated faith with what we are believing. The point that I am getting at is that faith is also associated with yielding.

The Bible says that even demons believe and tremble. That is not the God kind of faith because they are disobedient. I do not associate that kind of believing with faith. There is something associated with faith that relates to yieldedness. Faith is associated with yielding to God even as we believe. Many have taken the surface part of faith and kept it at this place of just believing. What I realize is that people can believe certain things and still will not do the right thing. Therefore, faith is closely related to yieldedness as well as believing. Sometimes believing something will not accomplish many things.

As I mentioned earlier, demons believe and tremble but they are not obedient or willfully yielded to God to do and fulfill His will. Have faith and be yielded to the will, desire, and intent of God. Faith comes by hearing and hearing by the Word of God. You are in faith when God declares or says something and you yield to it. Yieldedness to God will produce action.

Just believing is one level where it is very superficial because devils also believe, but do not obey. We believe and still may not do what we believe. If we believe certain things are right and we still do not do them, it is not faith because faith is seen action. *"Faith without works is dead"* (James 2:20 KJV). It births from something that comes out from God and then we yield to it. *"So you see, we are shown to be right with God by what we do, not by faith alone"* (James 2:24 NLT).

Jesus walked completely in faith because He was completely yielded to God. He walked completely in faith in every action, but it was related to what He saw His Father do. He only did what He saw His Father do. That is faith. Faith is birthed as it relates out of the will of God, not from what I can get from God.

Faith relates to yieldedness to God so that means that the things that God has spoken to me, I will yield to Him and obey. Faith is going to produce some great things in your life that comes by your yieldedness, not just believing alone. You can believe something and not do it, but when faith comes alive and you yield to it, it is about to produce something from God. In the following scripture, He gives Ezekiel a specific instruction. *"Then he said to me, Speak a prophetic message to these bones and say, 'Dry bones, listen to the word of the LORD'"* (Ezekiel 37:4 NLT)! Faith hears, yields,

84

and obeys.

In other words, "I'm going to do what God said." Some people try to work up the faith to speak to those dry bones. God says, "You don't work up any faith. You yield to my Word and those dry bones are going to respond because it was my will that those bones would respond."

The More You Yield,
The Greater God Uses You

If we do not allow God to take hold of us, we can forget about the dry bones moving and coming back together. As you flow with greater intimacy in God, you may know some situations in which you may need to speak to dry bones.

God's miracle power manifests when you let God take hold of you and you yield to Him. Let God take hold of you, first! That is how to cultivate the presence of God. Just say, "God, take hold of me." When you yield to God, there is exceeding strength and power! God does not need you to know everything. All He needs you to do is yield to Him.

Yield to God with the little that you know and more will be added to you from God." If you yield, God will mightily use you. If you are yielding more and more to God, you are going to be used greater and greater by God. There is not a person that can hold you down. No one but yourself can stop you from yielding to God. You will be seeing some things as you are yielding to God that no one else sees.

Something happens when you yield to God. If a father wants deliverance from abusing or misusing women, in repentance he must pray for that and cry out to the Lord for it. Change does not come by only believing, but comes by yielding to God's Word concerning a situation. When you yield to something, it is what you become. When you yield to God, change will happen. When yielding to Him, you are becoming more like Him; you are seeing like Him.

God Will Test You for Tenderness & Yieldedness Before He Gives You An Assignment to Use You Mightily

When God talks to you, answer Him with a tender and yielded heart. Then you will pass His test for promotion to be used mightily by Him. You must be yielded to God so you can see like Him. Likewise, God took hold of Ezekiel and he saw. *"He led me all around among the bones that covered the valley floor. They were scattered everywhere across the ground and were completely dried out. Then he asked me, 'Son of man, can these bones become living people again'"* (Ezekiel 37:2-3 NLT)?

Something is happening when God is asking you questions that relate to His will. It is not the questions like, "Son, why do you do this? Why are you acting like that?" I am not referring to questions like that. In other words, God is saying, "I'm getting ready to do something greater than you know. Son of man, can those bones live?" When God starts talking to you like that, answer with a tender and yielded heart.

Look at the yieldedness of Ezekiel. Most people would have answered, "Yes, those bones can live." Ezekiel did not go there. He said, "Lord, only you know if those bones can live." In other words, he did not go before God. He did not presume. He was not all knowledgeable. He did not say, "Well God, I have seen you do it one-thousand times before." With tenderness and yieldedness, he said, "I don't know Lord! Only you know!"

Because of his yielded heart, God promoted Ezekiel. In

86

other words, God's response was, "Right answer, we're getting ready to do something right now. I can use you! Now, your words and tongue can become what I'm about to do here in the earth." The scripture says, *"Then he said to me, 'Speak a prophetic message to these bones and say, Dry bones, listen to the word of the LORD'"* (Ezekiel 37:4 NLT)! As you yield to God, your voice will become the voice of life, and bring change even to situations and to nations and generations.

Miracles Happen When You Pray With Expectation & Put Value on It

When you pray with expectation, you expect to see prayer results as you put value on what you pray and see that it is important. Then, God will hear your prayer, and you will move in realms of the supernatural glory and power of God. On the other hand, God does not hear your prayer if you pray with the wrong motive, such as with religious performance.

Let me give some examples of wrong motive prayers. When we pray, we are not just praying out to open spaces. We are not showing off or showing people that we can pray a certain way in order to make a good impression to be accepted by them. We are not pretending to pray. Our prayers will not go up into the atmosphere because God only hears the prayers of purity—prayers that are sincere and with all our hearts. The Bible says that He hears the prayers of the righteous.

We are moving into a place where we can be trusted. God says, "If you pray into a situation, I'm going to respond and do some things." When you pray, you cannot reflect on your past failure or lack of prayer results. It does not matter what happened in the past; you are in a different place. No matter what happened in that place, you should have an expectation about things that are happening now and will happen in the future. When God moves, peace manifests within us, God speaks to us, and we get answers. There is an assurance that comes in yieldedness and intimacy in God. That is why it is so critical to cultivate that environment. No matter what happens, you still want that environment where God dwells.

God can give people a specific word of knowledge or prophecy in a particular time when the atmosphere is right for people to get that word from God. Then, when they speak it at that right time, suddenly, people will be healed and miracles will occur. I believe in miracles. Signs, wonders, and miracles are important today! If you do not put a value on your prayer, you will not see them work in your life, church, or ministry.

If we minimize it, treat it with disrespect, and do not put a value on it, we will not see the miracles move in our lives and ministries. We will not see it follow us. If it is not important to us, God will not use us in it and He will not let us see signs, wonders, and miracles. We must put a value on what God values. The Holy Spirit will take preeminence in your life as you yield and value the things of God.

Then, when you speak, God is breathing into the situation, and the breath of God brings life. *"Then he said to me, Speak a prophetic message to these bones and say, Dry bones, listen to the word of the LORD! This is what the Sovereign LORD says: Look! I am going to put breath into you and make you live again! I will put flesh and muscles on you and cover you with skin. I will put breath into you, and you will come to life ... "* (Ezekiel 37:4-6 NLT).

Therefore, you must be careful with the words you speak. When you begin to speak pure words—God words—God breathes life into your words. On the contrary, if you speak negatively about people or leadership, even when you do not know full details, then you are speaking judgment, which may come back on you.

For this reason, you must not say negative things over a man in governmental authority, whether you like that person or not. Because you respect God's Word, you guard your words for you know that there is something about honoring people in positions of authority. God's word says that all authority comes from God (Romans 13:1). God is not going to allow you to have a God-breathed word if you do not value authority and leadership and honor them. When God speaks, that is when you speak a God-breathed word. Therefore, you need a God-breathed word that changes things and brings the life of God to every situation.

Let's Pray

"Heavenly, Father, I am honoring you so much for your mighty presence. I declare today that I love you. I value you. You are so important. I delight in praising you. You are the important part of my life. I come in your mighty name; may it forever be exalted. May it forever be magnified. Breathe on me Lord, even right now. Holy Spirit, breathe upon me. Today, I invite you to breathe upon my worship, praise, prayer, and the sharing of the gospel when I speak to others about you. As David said, don't take your presence from me. Father, I bless you and honor you in a tremendous way, right now. I pray for fathers and for our nation. I pray for men in my family and church, and the churches of this city, state, and my nation. God breathe upon them today. Lord, give them the right spirit, the spirit of obedience that they will not model out what is in the market or society.

"Right now, I pray that they take their lead, and full authority as godly men with purity of heart. Just with them showing up, your presence is going to be there. Things are going to turn about just because they are going to be examples. If they never say another word, just your presence will speak volumes through them. Thank you for the men that carry God's presence in my home, family, church, and the churches of this city.

"I pray that they will no longer hide or make excuses. God, I pray that they step forward and examine their own heart. Look upon their lives as you have never looked upon them before. I declare that they will not hide anything from you, Lord, because truly they cannot hide from you. Examine them. If they are elders, right now, make them the elders that you called them to be. If they are deacons, right now, make them the deacons that you called them to be. If they are leaders, make them the leaders you called them to be.

"If they are pastors, right now, make them pastors that are pleasing to your heart. Make them pastors that you would delight in them. Whatever they are, Lord, if they are a member of the Body of Christ, I ask you to make them greater examples to everyone who comes through the doors of their churches and to the people of their nation.

"Thank you Father for the young people who will show forth and begin to display what really should be displayed. In Jesus' name, I declare that they do not respond to peer pressure. They are going to begin to live lives that pleases you. Someone is going to see it. Somebody is going to be attracted to it and say, 'Do you know what? That's the way it should be and that it is the right example to follow.' Thank you for it now, Father. With every word that these men and women begin to declare, let it be God-breathed. Let every song begin to be God-breathed. Let every exhortation be God-breathed; let it be God-inspired. Let every prayer be God-breathed and God-inspired. Thank you for it Father. I give you all the praise and glory in Jesus' Name, Amen."

CHAPTER 6
BUILDING
GOD'S HOUSE

"You are coming to Christ, who is the living cornerstone of God's temple. He was rejected by people, but he was chosen by God for great honor. And you are living stones that God is building into his spiritual temple. What's more, you are his holy priests. Through the mediation of Jesus Christ, you offer spiritual sacrifices that please God."

I Peter 2:4-5 (NLT)

You are the temple that God is building for a holy habitation. In everything a believer thinks, says, and does in the challenges, trials, and temptations of life, he is building his temple for God. If you are serious with God, He will give you specific instructions to build your temple as God's habitation. You are the temple of the Holy Ghost. You are the temple that is being built.

Today is the time to get your heart on fire for God and make the right choices to build your temple. Right now and every day of your life, God is giving opportunity to build your temple based on your devotion to God, which only God can see in your heart.

If you want God's mighty manifested presence and power to flow in and through you, it is essential to build your temple according to His instructions and be willing to obey His Word.

In this chapter, I want to challenge you in how to be

serious in building your temple, how to prepare the secrets of your heart devotion to God, and how to make sure you are at one with God. You must examine your heart devotion to God. You must examine how your devotion and responses to life's challenges will show in every part of your daily life.

When serious about building your temple for God, He is serious about finishing it correctly. If there is ever a time you must be willing to sacrifice your desires for God's desires and get serious about building the temple of your heart for God, it is now! That is why I encourage you to read this chapter and put it into practice.

Season to Keep Your Hearts Right With God

This is the season to keep your heart right with God. We have to work with each other in faith like we have never worked before. We have to get out of our comfort zones. We must come out of our nucleus of friends and wrong thinking that says, "It's just us, we know God, and no one knows God like us." We have to come out of that because while we are messing around, people are serious about winning this generation to their religion.

You must make every effort to go out of your comfort zone. Make every effort to get out of your nucleus of people that only think your way. Stop thinking that if no one thinks your way, then he or she is not a part of the family of God.

Instead, focus on how our God is so vast and incredible. If it were not for His mercy, we would not fit into His nucleus. Focus on that! If it was not for His mercy, we would not fit into Heaven, but He made the way. There was a sacrifice that was needed, and He said, "I'll be the sacrifice."

Season to Be Filled
With Fresh Fire & Power

This is the season to be filled with God's fire as the believers in the book of Acts. In seasons past, people were hungry for God and they were saved and filled with the Holy Ghost! In this hour, many people can join a church, say they are Christians, and never see a real manifestation of God's power in their lives. Many lost the fire that the people had in the day of the early church when people were born into the family of God, filled with the Spirit of God, and the power of God began to operate in their lives.

In this hour, many people are not baptized in the Holy Spirit. Many take it lightly and because of pride, they think they are mature, and do not have to operate that way anymore. Many think that their church is so mature that they are no longer emotional. Some think they have grown up.

In the book of Acts, they were emotional and full of the power of God. However, if we have grown up, then we should have more power. When they prayed, the foundations of the building shook because the Holy Spirit was powerfully present.

Today, many churches and people think they are so mature but they lack the power. In the body of Christ, now is the time to get back on fire for God. When you are on fire, not only will you come in the church and join it, but you will be surrendered and completely yielded to God, be wholly given over to God, and used by Him mightily.

Instead of living your life just to manage sin and keep it under control, now is the time to live holy by giving yourself completely over to God, and living your life being thrust into His presence and glory.

Agree With God
To Walk in Victory

However, while the church is busy managing its sin, someone is serious about winning this world and taking God out of it. People say, "Lord, keep me from this and that, keep my mind from this or that way," but Jesus Christ said that He has already given us the victory. The Bible says that He always causes us to triumph in Christ Jesus (II Corinthians 2:2-14 KJV). The Bible does not lie, so if we are not victorious, there is something we need to examine about us. God is raising you to understand how He walks and what He desires. If God said, "I always cause you to triumph," then, the least that I can do is agree with His Word.

We could say, "God, I don't know how that works and operates, but I agree with you." If we agree with God, this forces us to move away from the edge of living in sin and defeat. If people do not completely surrender to God, they will say, "I'm not going to sin, but I'm going to stay close to it. I'm not going to do outward things, but I'm going to be there on the edge."

As you live the life of letting Jesus cause you to triumph, He will always cause you to move away from the edge. When you have pure heart, you purpose in your mind and heart that you are not going to walk close to the edge. Therefore, others may walk close to the edge and play around with sin, but not us. The reason is that we want God to be fully living in our temples—a place where He is delighted and pleased to live and dwells in us and through us.

God desires His presence and fire to dwell inside of you, and that fire will not be present if you are playing close to the edge in sin. God's fire does not come by being close to the edge, but by being close to the Holy One. Therefore, as the

94

fire is stirred inside, you will breakthrough to another dimension. Other people will even come off the edge when you are staying close to Holy One.

Actually, the edge should not be familiar to you, but it should be strange. Unfortunately, we live in a time when God is strange to many people. There is power in living close in God's presence—intimately in Him and Him in you! If you have been struggling with some things, and start to pray for deliverance, it will happen because you are not playing with living on the edge. God is drawing you into His presence and glory. God is revitalizing your life and wants to draw you to Himself. You should never be able to live without Him!

Season to Be Willing to Sacrifice
Your Self-Desires for God-Desires

This is the season to sacrifice self-desires in exchange for God-desires, and the time for effectiveness and willingness to sacrifice. Not everyone is going to be effective, but to be effective relates to you doing something in your life. The willingness to sacrifice does not mean that you have to do away with this or that, but it means that you sacrifice yourself to God. When you know the correlation, you are willing to give yourself as living sacrifice to God. Jesus said, *"Not my will but thy will be done."*

The willingness to sacrifice is not going to be struggle of thinking that you have to do away with this or that. No, it is going to be you who becomes the living sacrifice. You who are willing will become a sacrifice because you know the season and timing—right now, you know what is happening, and that God is preparing things for you.

In other words, the Bible says, *"And so, dear brothers and sisters, I plead with you to give your bodies to God*

95

because of all he has done for you. Let them be a living and holy sacrifice--the kind he will find acceptable. This is truly the way to worship him. Don't copy the behavior and customs of this world, but let God transform you into a new person by changing the way you think. Then you will learn to know God's will for you, which is good and pleasing and perfect" (Romans 12:1-2 NLT).

Your Devotion to God
Will Show In Your Daily Life

Your devotion to God will show in all areas of your daily life. The sacrifice will work by your devotion. When I am referring to devotion, I am not talking merely about the time you are getting up to pray. It is more than coming to prayer to increase your prayer life.

Your devotion to God will show in your marriage, business, relationships, and in your surrender to the Lord. Your devotion to God will show in your yielding to authority. Your devotion to God will show in your brokenness. Your devotion to God shows by how you respond to people. Your devotion to God will show by not harboring offense in your heart. Your devotion to God will show in your surrender to the Holy Spirit.

Your devotion to God will show when you rid yourself of unforgiveness. In fact, your devotion shows God that you are serious when no one else understands what is happening on the inside of you. At that point, it is only between God and you, because people will not see the death that you are going through.

Therefore, people will not see the willing sacrifice that you are making on the inside. Men cannot see and honor it, but only God can see your heart and honor it. He says, "What you do in secret, I'm going to honor it before you!" That is what it means to go into the secret place—making decisions in your heart that honor God.

You Need to Be Serious
About Building God's Temple

When you are serious with God, you will be serious about building God's temple. David told his son Solomon that God chose him to build God's Temple—His sanctuary. It says, *"And Solomon, my son, learn to know the God of your ancestors intimately. Worship and serve him with your whole heart and a willing mind. For the LORD sees every heart and knows every plan and thought. If you seek him, you will find him. But if you forsake him, he will reject you forever. So take this seriously. The LORD has chosen you to build a Temple as his sanctuary. Be strong, and do the work"* (I Chronicles 28:9-10 NLT).

God's Word alone is truth and He never has to say that you need to take it seriously because there is enough power in the Word itself. Anytime God says to take something seriously, it is wisdom to do it! David told his son, "Begin to get serious because you are about to build the sanctuary of God. So get serious!" Then he says this, "Be strong and do the work!" In that time, he was building a physical building for the house of God. However, in our time, we are the temple of God and He is saying, "Get serious. You are the temple of the Holy Ghost. Get serious and begin to build your temple! Begin to build this sanctuary!"

What is awesome is that however you build it, is how it is going to look. Therefore, you need to examine what you are building and how you are building it. You have the ability to defile the temple. On the other hand, you have the ability to consecrate your temple to God. The Bible says that you are co-laborers with Christ, and He is the foundation in which all things are built. God says, "I'll build the foundation, but I have ordained that you build the temple."

David Was Serious
To Build God's Temple

I want to show you how serious David was with the preparation to build the sanctuary. It says, *"Then David gave Solomon the plans for the Temple and its surroundings, including the entry room, the storerooms, the upstairs rooms, the inner rooms, and the inner sanctuary—which was the place of atonement"* (Verse 11 NLT).

David was serious about preparing for the sanctuary. He was serious about all the things that he began to do in preparing for it. Like David, you must be serious in your walk with God. We cannot live our lives half-heartedly and be influenced by every wind that comes or by everything that happens, or by our circumstances and by what another is or is not doing. Many people are building their temples.

In the scripture, we are going to find that David was so exact and accurate that he did not only focus on building the temple, but also the precious stones that were going into the temple and this is incredible to me.

God Made You to Be
At One With Him

You need to keep your heart pure by being at one with God. David made plans to build all those rooms, but with one room in particular, no one could get in that room which he called the inner sanctuary. With your temple, no one can get in your inner sanctuary because you are protected. There is only one who can get there, and He is the Almighty God. He is the only one who can get into that sanctuary. On the other hand, if people have offense or unforgiveness in their hearts, they can let someone else in that sanctuary. If they have ought against someone, it is not on the outside, but it is within the inner sanctuary.

The inner sanctuary is only designed for atonement, which means you are "at—one—ment" with God. The inner sanctuary is only built for you to be at one with God. Therefore, at all costs, you must protect the inner sanctuary so that no one can get into it. That is why if offense comes in, you must quickly get rid of it because it is a place of atonement, a place of oneness with God.

The Hand of God
Wrote Specific Instructions
To Build the Temple

When you are serious, God will reveal His specific plans to build your temple and when you know the specific plans for God's temple, you will do exactly what God says. David was serious and gave specific instructions to Solomon. The Bible says, *"David also gave Solomon all the plans he had in mind for the courtyards of the LORD's Temple, the outside rooms, the treasuries, and the rooms for the gifts dedicated to the LORD. The king also gave Solomon the instructions concerning the work of the various divisions of priests and Levites in the Temple of the LORD. And he gave specifications for the items in the Temple that were to be used for worship"* (Verses 12-13 NLT).

David was serious. He did not stop there, but he was determined he would obey God with all his heart. Therefore, he proceeds with the specific instructions of gold needed for service, and lampstands, lamps, and silver for the lampstands. He continues, *"David gave instructions regarding how much gold and silver should be used to make the items needed for service. He told Solomon the amount of gold needed for the gold lampstands and lamps, and the amount of silver for the silver lampstands, depending on how each would be used"* (Verses 14-15 NLT).

David was determined he would not leave out any designated plans. He continued to share the specific instructions of gold needed for the table on which the Bread of the Presence would be placed, and silver needed for other tables. It says, *"He designated the amount of gold for the table on which the Bread of the Presence would be placed and the amount of silver for other tables"* (Verse 16 NLT).

David designated the amount of gold and silver needed for certain items. It says, *"David also designated the amount of gold for the solid gold meat hooks used to handle the sacrificial meat and for the basins, pitchers, and dishes, as well as the amount of silver for every dish"* (Verse 17 NLT).

In conclusion, David designated the amount of gold for the altar of incense and gave to Solomon the plan of God for the Lord's chariot, the gold cherubim. The scripture says, *"He designated the amount of refined gold for the altar of incense. Finally, he gave him a plan for the LORD's 'chariot"—the gold cherubim. 'Every part of this plan,' David told Solomon, 'was given to me in writing from the hand of the LORD'"* (Verses 18-19 NLT).

Guard Your Heart— Your Inner Sanctuary, Out of It Are the Issues of Life

God gave David a specific plan to build God's Temple! In relation to building our temples, God is specific about our temples and we cannot live haphazard lives! We have to be focused and determined because there are forces that are trying to get into our inner sanctuary. Actually, these forces are not only trying to build the temple for us, but in building it, they are trying to defile it.

We have to watch seriously our inner sanctuary. We must be focused and determined, and understand what God is building. We are not just a Christian who goes to church, but God is actually building a habitation for Him to dwell within us.

Therefore, you must be serious because you are the habitation that God is building so He can dwell within you, and not just here on earth, but for eternity. You must be serious because the only ones who will be in Heaven are those who have been built in the habitation of God. Salvation is free but it will cost something for you to live this life for real. It cost Jesus His life and it will cost you your life as you die to self that Christ may live in and through you.

To be Courageous,
"God Is With Us"
Is the Mindset You Need

God's Word is the right mindset that causes you to stay focused on Jesus and overcome all obstacles. In doing the work of the Lord, when you are strong and courageous, know that He will never fail you or forsake you. He is always with you and you will be victorious in daily life.

Again, David gave the same encouragement to remind Solomon to be strong, courageous, and do the work. It says, *"Then David continued, 'Be strong and courageous, and do the work. Don't be afraid or discouraged, for the LORD God, my God, is with you. He will not fail you or forsake you. He will see to it that all the work related to the Temple of the*

LORD is finished correctly" (Verse 20 NLT). This is important because if we do not have this mindset, we will slip back and allow anything to come into our lives.

As David encouraged his son, likewise, God is encouraging us to be strong. David is encouraging his son. David represents God and Solomon represents his son, the children of God. He is encouraging us to be strong, do the work, and be courageous. That means, when things start to come at you, be strong enough to say, "No, not here. My heart is good ground for God and not for just anything that comes along."

You have to be strong enough and when the people talk about you and say you are "holier than thou" and all those kinds of things that people say, you have to be strong. In addition to that, you have to be courageous when they are convicted and say, "What's wrong with me?" You must understand that with everything happening in life, you are building your temple.

All you need to know is that God is with you. Therefore, "Lord, you don't even need to explain everything to me. You do not have to explain it all to me. Just let me know that you are with me. That is all that I need to know. Then God, you will make your will manifest and show me your desires. You're not only going to show me my heart; you're going to demonstrate your presence."

If Serious About Building
Your Temple for God, He is Serious
By Finishing It Correctly

When you are building your temple for God, remember that God will finish the work correctly! David said, *"He will not fail you or forsake you. He will see to it that all the work*

related to the Temple of the LORD is finished correctly"
(Verse 20 NLT). That is God's promise to us. In other words,
he was saying, "God promised me that He would finish the
work correctly."

The only thing that He is asking is that you understand
you are building a temple for Him. Because you have that
understanding, you are aware of what you allow to happen
around you and in you. God says, "If you do that and you're
not haphazard about it, and if you're serious about it, I'm
serious about letting you know that I'm going to build it
correctly! It is going to be finished correctly! It is going to be
done correctly!" Therefore, you already know the end that as
you are building, you are not going to end up just any kind of
way, but God is going to finish it correctly.

Moreover, God is telling us that the work is enormous,
but God will finish it correctly. The scripture says, *"Then
King David turned to the entire assembly and said, 'My son
Solomon, whom God has clearly chosen as the next king of
Israel, is still young and inexperienced. The work ahead of
him is enormous, for the Temple he will build is not for mere
mortals—it is for the LORD God himself'"* (I Chronicles 29:1
NLT)!

Clearly, God has chosen you! Even though you may be
young and inexperienced, if you don't know all about it, and
don't know how you are going to do it, He keeps reminding
you to be strong, be courageous and do the work.

You must never think that walking and living a Christian
life is a light thing. God is saying, "The work ahead of you is
enormous. There's some serious decisions that you're
making as you're building this temple. The work is
enormous. It is bigger than you are able to build, but I will
finish it correctly. Can you just do what I say?"

You must do what God says and He will be serious to finish your temple. The instructions were clearly defined when God was telling David, "Do what I say, David. You don't know how to do the temple, but do what I say and I'll finish it correctly!" Then, the scripture says, *"... The work ahead of Solomon is enormous, for the Temple he will build is not for mere mortals—it is for the Lord God himself"* (I Chronicles 29:1 NLT)!

You may not see yourself that way, but God is saying that the temple you are building is not for mere mortals, but it is for God Himself. This is serious.

In whatever you do, when you get your instruction from God, you will not fail, but God will be with you to complete the work. You must use every resource at your command. David says, *"Using every resource at my command, I have gathered as much as I could for building the Temple of my God. Now there is enough gold, silver, bronze, iron, and wood, as well as great quantities of onyx, other precious stones, costly jewels, and all kinds of fine stone and marble"* (Verse 2 NLT).

There will be abundant supply when you get your instructions from God. For this reason, it is important that you get the instructions from God. That is why it is important for you to be in church and have Pastors and leaders teach you. David said, "I use every resource to build this temple at my command."

Build Your Temple
Based on Your Devotion to God
And by What You Do in Secret

When you are serious with God, you give all of your heart to Him. You build your temple by what you do in secret before God and that is your devotion! The secret treasures—the sincere devotion of your heart belongs to Him. David said that he gave all his private treasures of gold and silver to help with the construction of the Temple. He said this as follows: *"And now, because of my devotion to the Temple of my God, I am giving all of my own private treasures of gold and silver to help in the construction. This is in addition to the building materials I have already collected for his holy Temple"* (Verse 3 NLT).

In addition to the building materials that David already collected for God's Holy Temple, he was giving all of his private treasure of gold and silver because of his devotion to God. David said, "I prepared everything needed to build the temple." Everything David prepared was of quality. Some things were of higher quality, such as *"... gold, silver, bronze, iron, and wood, as well as great quantities of onyx, other precious stones, costly jewels, and all kinds of fine stone and marble."*

David gave all of the following high quality treasures and donated them to the building of God's temple: *"I am donating more than 112 tons of gold from Ophir and 262 tons of refined silver to be used for overlaying the walls of the buildings and for the other gold and silver work to be done by the craftsmen. Now then, who will follow my example and give offerings to the LORD today"* (Verse 4 NLT)?

Notice that he did not give a little portion of what was valuable to him, but he gave all of the things that were of high value to him. The 112 tons of gold is not something minor. It was evidence that he was taking the temple seriously.

Furthermore, he added 262 tons of refined silver to be used to overlay the walls of the building. That is an awesome scripture. David talks about others following his example to give offerings to the Lord. Whose example are we following and who is following our example? David was giving all of his own private treasures out of his devotion to God.

Two things happened because of David's devotion to God. The first thing is that God gave him specific instructions on how to build. The second thing is that He gave them the resources needed to build. The giving of his own private treasure related to his devotion to God.

For this reason, it is important for you to examine your level of devotion to God. Devotion to God is not just praying, but it is genuine obedience to God from the inner man.

Devotion relates to that secret thing between you and God. When no one else knows about it, you are wholly devoted to Him in secret. That is where devotion comes in. Devotion can be your response to a person, or how you want to respond, but you do not respond. Devotion to God is how you want to do something, but because you are devoted to God, you will not do it. Real intimacy with God and in God is a devoted heart.

Your secret decisions that you devote to God is what He sees. People may see the outward religious devotion where you are praying all the time, paying your tithes or doing good religious works, but they cannot see the inner choice that you make to serve God. This is when the things of gold, silver, and the costly gems are being added to your life. Only God sees the things you do in secret.

Focus on Your Reward in Heaven
With Your Responses to Life's Challenges

You must see that your reward is in Heaven and this must be your focus when doing secret things that God sees. No one can see your inward devotion to God, but your reward is in Heaven, and when you get to Heaven, you are going to be wearing costly jewels. You are going to be wearing gold and silver and yours is not going to fit anyone else. Yours is going to be unique, just for us, because it will be related to your unique trials, tribulations, and challenges that you went through, and in the midst of them, you stayed devoted to God. Paul said, there is a crown of righteousness laid up for you.

God is building a tabernacle in which He will inhabit and your choices are related to it. That is why I ask, "What do you look like now and what are you building?" Your choices relate to the costly gems being added to your life. In those challenging moments and times, people will look at you and say, "I don't know how you do that; there is no way you can do that." You can say, "Well, you don't understand, some jewels are being added to my life right now. I see the far end. I am not living for the moment. I am not living for the reward of man. I'm living for God."

Be Careful How You Build Your Temple

Whether or not you know it, you are building a habitation for God to dwell. In the Bible, Paul said that you must be very careful when you are building it and lay it like an expert builder. Paul said, *"Because of God's grace to me, I have laid the foundation like an expert builder. Now others are building on it. But whoever is building on this foundation must be very careful. For no one can lay any foundation other than the one we already have—Jesus Christ"* (I Corinthians 3:10-11 NLT).

As I previously stated, Jesus is the foundation, but God has ordained that you build the temple. Just like it was in the

107

Old Testament, God did not build the temple but man had to build the temple. God is allowing you to be a co-laborer with Him in building this temple.

You must be careful not to build your foundation with wood, hay, and stubble because the fire of God will consume these things if they are the materials you have built upon. However, if you are building your foundation with jewels, precious stones, gold, and silver, it will stand. The Bible says, *"Anyone who builds on that foundation may use a variety of materials—gold, silver, jewels, wood, hay, or straw"* (Verse 12 NLT).

You must realize that your Christian life is that serious and God gives opportunities to build your temple. He will give you a design. That is why it is important you follow the instructions, and the design He gives you. Ultimately, you are building what it is going to look like in the end. I do not want to build with wood, straw, and hay. Offense is an example of building with straw. Your wife, husband, or friend may not even know that they offended you and six months down the road, you are still offended. That is an example of building with straw and hay. Get it right with God and with them. When you forgive, you are building with precious gems.

If Your Work Survives the Fire, You Will Receive Your Reward in Heaven

The fire of God will expose the things in your heart foundation that is of God, and if the work survives, you will receive a reward. This says, *"But on the judgment day, fire will reveal what kind of work each builder has done. The fire will show if a person's work has any value. If the work survives, that builder will receive a reward"* (Verses 13-14 NLT). I love that scripture. Right now, you are not only adding jewels, but also, God says, "I am going to give you a

108

reward. You are building jewels, but I'm going to give you a crown." That crown is going to be made exactly for you. Every inch, minor detail, facet, and shaping of it is related to the life that you are living right now.

If Your Work Burns Up, You Will Suffer Great Loss & Barely Make It to Heaven

The Bible says that if the work survives, the builders get a reward, but if it is burned up, he will suffer great loss. *"But if the work is burned up, the builder will suffer great loss. The builder will be saved, but like someone barely escaping through a wall of flames"* (Verse 15 NLT). I do not want to go to Heaven like that. This is why we do not play with sin. We do not walk close to the lines. If we really knew what we are risking, we would not be close to the line.

When You Listen to God's Word & Obey It, You Are Building Your House on a Rock

You must examine if you build your foundation on the rock or the sand. In the Bible, Jesus talks about the wise and foolish builders. A man built his foundation on rock and another man built it on sand. This is important because the only moment you have is right now, but the next one is not guaranteed. For this reason, what you presently do is extremely important; it is the only moment that is guaranteed.

Jesus said, *"Anyone who listens to my teaching and follows it is wise, like a person who builds a house on solid rock"* (Matthew 7:24 NLT). As I said before, Jesus is saying, "Do what I say! Just follow my instructions. I'm going to finish this correctly!" It is not easy, but if you obey Him, He will finish it correctly. He said, "The work is enormous, but if you do it, I'm going to finish it correctly!"

Everything in life is about you building a foundation. In every thing that concerns your life, God has created you to be a builder. If you are not yet married, you are building a relationship and you are building a future. You may be building a career, you may be building a house, or you may be building a business. It is not just the spiritual aspect of it; it is a natural process.

You are made to build, but nothing shall be built stronger, and nothing shall have your passion or compassion more than building the house of the Lord, which is you. Likewise is the person who builds his house on a solid rock. The Bible says, *"Though the rain comes in torrents and the flood waters rise and the winds beat against that house, it won't collapse because it is built on bedrock. But anyone who hears my teachings and doesn't obey it is foolish, like a person who builds a house on sand. When the rains and floods come and the winds beat against that house, it will collapse with a mighty crash"* (Verses 25-27 NLT).

Daily, you are going to get some opportunities to build your temple. You will get opportunities to build gold and jewels in your temple. If you are of age and God has not given you a mate, it is a challenge for single people to be kept by God. You will not be able to keep yourself if God does not keep you. However, when you agree with God in the keeping process, that is when the jewels, gold, and silver are being added to your life. Costly gems are being added and again, no one knows that you are secretly obeying God.

God's Presence Manifests
As You Build Your Temple
According to His Instructions

God's manifested presence will be in you, on you, and flow through you as you build your temple by His instructions. You need to see the result of what you are building. After Solomon completed everything he was to do, the Lord appeared to Solomon: *"So Solomon finished building the Temple of the LORD, as well as the royal palace. He completed everything he had planned to do. Then, the LORD appeared to Solomon a second time, as he had done before at Gibeon"* (I Kings 9: 1-2 NLT).

In other words, you may want the Lord to appear before the work is done, but God is going to appear when the temple is built according to His instruction.

Therefore, as you are living your life and your focus and understanding is that God is building your temple, and as God sees that temple being built, His presence comes. God appeared to Solomon when the temple was complete. God will hear your prayers when you obey His instruction. Then, He will set you apart as Holy unto Him to be a place for His name to be honored forever. *"The LORD said to him, 'I have heard your prayer and your petition. I have set the Temple apart to be holy—this place you have built where my name will be honored forever. I will always watch over it, for it is dear to my heart'"* (Verse 3 NLT).

Right now, can God say that He heard your prayer and petition and has set your temple to be Holy? In other words, God is saying, "If you build this temple the way I'm telling you to build it, not only will My presence be there, but it is dear to My heart, and I will watch over it."

The other thing is that He is going to honor His name and that is very important. There are many times in the Bible when God says, "I'm going to honor My own name." Even if man does not honor it, God says, "I will honor My own name."

For that reason, praising God is important. Sometimes,

we do things based on how we feel. If we do not feel like honoring Him, He will not lose anything in that because if we do not honor Him, He will honor His own self. This is the reason why God is allowing you to build the temple so He can put Himself in you. Therefore, when we do not feel like honoring God, He will honor Himself in us. That is incredible! When you do not feel like praising Him, something will stir on the inside of you and if the Holy Spirit is there, God Himself will begin to magnify His own name. In fact, He does things only because of His name.

In some of the blessings you are walking in right now, you must know that He is honoring His name. He says, "It is not because you are special, but it's because I made a promise to Abraham. I'm going to honor My name in what I said to Abraham." You're blessed because God honors His promise to Abraham. "I'm going to bless you and it has nothing to do with you." God is incredible!

Therefore, in that place when you think you cannot do it, God said, "It's alright; I'll honor My own name." That is a wonderful strategy and this is why He says, "If you do what I say, I will finish the temple correctly because you don't know that the temple you're building is not for mere mortals, but I myself will honor My temple. When you can't, I'm going to honor My name." For this reason, you will be kept because God is going to honor His name in your temple. You are the temple of the Holy Spirit!

You cannot build your temple by your own power or ability, but it takes yielding to the Holy Spirit and letting Him take control. The Bible says, *"Then he said to me, 'This is what the LORD says to Zerubbabel: It is not by force nor by strength, but by my Spirit, says the LORD of Heaven's Armies. Nothing, not even a mighty mountain, will stand in Zerubbabel's way: it will become a level plain before him! And when Zerubbabel sets the final stone of the Temple in the place, the people will shout: 'May God bless it! May God bless it!' Then another message came to me from the LORD: 'Zerubbabel is the one who laid the foundation of the Temple, and he will complete it. Then you will know that the LORD of Heaven's Armies has sent me. Do not despise these small beginnings, for the LORD rejoices to see the work begin, to see the plumb line in Zerubbabel's hand"* (Zechariah 4:6-10 NLT).

In other words, the Lord is saying, "You don't have to figure out this thing and do it; I rejoice in just seeing the work begin." It does not matter the many times you failed yesterday or even this very moment. God says, "Do not despise small beginnings. I rejoice in seeing the work begin. Just begin to work. Just start the process." Get up and get busy building the temple of God which is you.

God is telling you to be strong and get on with the rebuilding of your temple. The scripture continues, *"But now, I will not treat the remnant of my people as I treated them before, says the LORD of Heaven's Armies. For I am planting seeds of peace and prosperity among you. The grapevines will be heavy with fruit. The earth will produce its crops, and the heavens will release the dew. Once more I will cause the remnant in Judah and Israel to inherit these blessings. Among the other nations, Judah and Israel became symbols of a cursed nation. But no longer! Now I will rescue you and make you both a symbol and a source of blessing. So don't be afraid. Be strong, and get on with rebuilding the Temple"* (Zechariah 8:11-13 NLT)!

Today, make your decision that from this day forward, you will be serious to completely yield to the Holy Spirit and allow Him to be your leader. As you follow Him, He will cause you to do God's Word and build your temple to please God. The scripture says, *"You are coming to Christ, who is the Living Cornerstone of God's temple... You are living stones that God is building into His spiritual temple. What's more, you are His holy priests. Through the mediation of Jesus Christ, you offer spiritual sacrifices that please God"* (I Peter 2:4-5 NLT).

In conclusion, I want to encourage you to be strong and courageous in everything as you rebuild the temple of God. Make sure your foundation is based on God's Word. Your inward choices are your devotion to God and when you choose to do God's will with a pure, willing, and obedient heart, the presence of God will manifest in and through you to bring others to Jesus.

Right now, you are determining your eternal destiny in Heaven. As you build your house, God will eternally reward you with precious jewels and precious stones, a crown of righteousness; but even that does not compare with real precious intimacy in God!

Yield to the Holy Spirit
With Fresh Surrender to Him
Pray With Me

"Holy Spirit, Spirit of Life, Spirit of power, Spirit of truth, I appreciate you so much. I love you so much. I yield afresh to you. Take preeminence over my life. I thank you for being the Paraclete, the one that comes to stand alongside. I thank you for revealing Jesus in an awesome way. I thank you for magnifying and glorifying His name. I declare that you are awesome, you are great, and you are my God. Help me to yield and surrender to you, even more.

"I don't want to do anything without you. I want to acknowledge you. You are the One that leads my life. You are the one that glorifies the name of Jesus. You are the one full of power, full of might, and full of strength. I can do nothing without you. I surrender even more of myself unto you. I yield to you now Holy Spirit, do what you desire. Be pleased in all I say and do. Reveal Jesus in a greater way to me. Help my life to be transformed and changed into your image. I thank you that you are my Savior, deliverer, and healer of my body.

"Lord, I am complete in you. I give you your liberty and freedom. Clear me from the mindset of religion that would hinder me from doing your complete will. Clear me from my past experiences that said you could only do things in a certain way.

"I am new today and fresh by your presence. Lord, I am not trusting in anything of the past. You are fresh every morning, because you are new every day! Great is your faithfulness towards me. Lord, thank you for revealing yourself like I have never seen you before. Cause me to be like a little child that I will be excited about you again. I bless you for it and give you praise in Jesus name. Amen."

CHAPTER 7
THE ABIDING GLORY

"... Your godliness will lead you forward and the glory of the Lord will protect you from behind."

Isaiah 58:8 (NLT)

This is the season to learn how to pray to see God's glory and carry God's presence, and His heart by developing intimacy with Him through prayer. To have God's presence and glory should be more valuable to you than any other person or thing on earth. You can be a daily carrier of God's glory. If you want His abiding Glory in a powerful way, this chapter will challenge you how to surrender to God with the right purpose as the most important thing in your life, and go after God's presence to be filled with godliness and holiness.

God's Word promises that as you have the right spirit to give yourself completely over to Him through intimacy in God, He will speedily respond when you call on His name. In addition, I will share the importance of right heart attitudes that brings quick healing and restoration results in your life.

Learn how to come with purity of heart that brings God's glory, safety, and promotion in your life. You will read how children, young people, and adults can keep purity of heart so they can be filled with God's glory, and not allow the devil to steal purity out of their hearts. Understand how to make this your season to have intimacy with God so that you can hear God, know how He thinks, responds to things He likes, and then obey Him. I will share how to have a right spirit that

117

seeks to know God's way, understand God more fully, and know Him for the sake of obedience and enjoying His favor. Learn how to go after God's glory with upmost respect and have His abiding goodness to favor you.

Season for the Abiding Glory

God wants His people to be in the abiding Glory and not going in and out with Him based on their particular situations and challenges. I believe there is a place of *"abiding in God, or abiding in Him."* In God's Word, Jesus says, *"If ye abide in me, and my words abide I in you* (John 15:7 KJV)." This means that we are abiding in God.

You have to know that you are a carrier of the glory of God. There is such a thing as the abiding glory that just stays. It does not come in and out. You do not have to work it up. You do not have to be with people. Some people cannot pray and get in there with God until a certain amount of people get in that place. However, God's plan is that you continually abide in His glory and I am going to show you how you can walk in that place.

Fasting Benefits Heart Attitudes
That Quickly Heals Your Wounds

There are heart attitudes that will cause salvation to come like the dawn and will quickly heal your wounds. In the following scriptures, God is telling us that if something is done, then this will happen; our salvation will come like the dawn. *"... this is the kind of fasting I want: Free those who are wrongly imprisoned; lighten the burden of those who work for you. Let the oppressed go free, and remove the chains that bind people. Share your food with the hungry, and give shelter to the homeless. Give clothes to those who need them, and do not hide from relatives who need your help. Then your salvation will come like the dawn, and your wounds will quickly heal"* (Isaiah 58:6-8 NLT).

When you have the right heart, your salvation will be like the dawn of the day. In the morning at dawn, it is amazing to see the sun come up. When it is completely dark, that edge of light comes up and the crest comes in and begins to light up that whole side of the earth. It is amazing and wonderful to see. If you have ever looked over the ocean and saw the sun, as it is coming up or even when it is going down, it is amazing. As soon as that part of the sun hits the edge, instantly, it begins to illuminate all areas. As it rises, it gets brighter and brighter. That is what God says will happen to you when you have the right heart and attitudes.

Brokenness: Key to Having
The Right Heart & Attitude

Let me clarify God's purpose and definition of a "fast" and His plan for brokenness, which is the key to having the right heart, and attitude that pleases God. He is saying that the real fast is not just sustaining from food, but it is having the right spirit; it is having the right heart.

As you have the right heart to do these things described in verses 6 through 8, your salvation will come like a dawn, and your wounds will heal quickly. God is saying that your healing will come quickly because out of the fast, you are being transformed with the right spirit and the right heart. As a result, there will be supernatural results.

The result of having a right heart is that it brings an inner healing inside of you, that just abstaining from food will not do. As you begin to be broken inside, it relates to the fasting. God is going to break you inside. As you begin to be broken,

119

you will start wanting to do the right things.

For this purpose of having a changed heart that desires to do the right things, you will set things in order. In the fast, God says that He wants you to begin to get those things in order, which were out of order. Some of them are small, but God says that He wants you to get it in order. He starts dealing with issues. He says that we need to start feeding the hungry. Instead of being hard on them, we are to start letting the oppressed go free.

Therefore, having the right spirit and right attitude is the kind of fast that God wants and is what you should want! As you come out of that fast, your salvation will come speedily. It will come like the dawn and your wounds will heal quickly. The result is that you are being healed emotionally. You are being healed from all those hurts, and all those past things that kept you in bondage and you are releasing things.

During the fast, these things should be happening. You are releasing things, God is cleaning the inner vessel, and the wounds of your body will begin to heal quickly.

Above all, the most important thing is to get your heart right with God. David prayed this, "Lord, create in me a clean heart, renew a right spirit within me, and then I can do the right things. Lord, teach me the transgressions of your ways." In other words, he wanted to get his heart clean and his spirit right because he could feel his spirit was not in order or right with God and it was off.

When you go into a fast, God begins to break things and show you things. Let God do that perfect work in you. Let Him fix the things that need fixing. Don't carry them for years. The fast is a surrender of your heart to God that says, "God, I'm giving myself to you and you are breaking things inside of me, so that I can have the right spirit and the right attitude to become a channel for the glory of God. When I speak, talk, minister, pray, dance or sing, or in whatever I do, I want my vessel to be pure."

By giving yourself to God for the reason of having a pure heart, He fills your heart with light and godliness will lead you to go forward into the plan and purpose of God. Light and purity penetrates darkness and purity comes from clean and undefiled vessels. *"... Godliness will lead you forward and the glory of the Lord will protect you from behind"* (Isaiah 58:8 NLT).

In other words, after you come off a fast and have a right spirit, you will not be led by your own decisions, what you think, and your ideas. You will be not be led by assumption, such as saying, "Well if I do it this way, then this will happen." Instead, your godliness will lead you forward. After you come out of the fast, your vessel is clean inside, and within your inner being, you are being led by your godliness!

Therefore, godliness leads you when you have a right heart and right spirit. Let me rephrase verse 8. God says, "When your godliness leads you, then I will be your rear guard. My glory will protect you from behind. You do not need to protect yourself from behind; you do not need to be watching over your shoulder. Your godliness is leading you and I will protect you from behind."

To sum it up, being in the hands of God must be your greatest desire. When you are in God's hands, He leads, guides, heals, and protects you, and answers your prayers. I want to be in the hands of God. That is all there is to it. I recognize I cannot protect myself; I cannot do it. God will have to stop some things. God is going to have to be my rear guard.

God promises that when you have the right spirit to give

yourself over to Him, you can call on the name of the Lord God and when you call, the Lord will answer, 'Yes, I am here. I will quickly reply; I will answer speedily." When I call, I want Him to reply quickly! That is God's promise! The scripture says, *"Then when you call, the LORD will answer. 'Yes, I am here,' he will quickly reply ..."* (Isaiah 58:9 NLT).

God's Glory, Safety & Promotion
Comes With Purity of Spirit

In the Bible, Paul is a godly example of a man who had a right spirit and God's glory. He heard God and received a clear and speedy answer or word from the Lord. While Paul was on a boat, he heard God. The boat was shipwrecked and the men on the boat were in turmoil. They knew that ship was going down. Then Paul said, "Everyone, an angel appeared to me today. Everyone is going to be spared."

The ship was going down, but everyone survived. Because he was in tune with God, He knew in advance the things that would happen. He had God's safety for himself and those with him. He and the men were spared because of Paul's right spirit and having God's glory.

Having the right spirit is important to know and hear God's voice, and understand what God reveals. Joseph was another godly example of a man with the right spirit. He was able to know and understand the things of God. In the Bible, the king found that Joseph was in prison; he came and took him out of it. He said, "We heard that you have wisdom and you are a young man. God gives you dreams and visions." The king did not tell him the dream, but Joseph heard it from the Lord.

Today, many people tell their dream, and because they do not have a right spirit to pray and get the interpretation, they would rather have someone to give the interpretation. The king did not tell the dream. He said, "If I am to know if it is God, you tell me the dream, and then give me the interpretation." Prior to this, Joseph endured all the trials and tribulations through prayer, and passed the test with a pure heart and right spirit. That is what brought him to his destiny.

To hear God's plans and move into your destiny, and have God's promotion, you must have a right spirit and godliness. That is what I like about Joseph. It did not say that he interpreted the dream. Instead, he prayed by saying, "God, show me the answer." The next day he came back and said, "Oh king, live. God has spoken to me."

After that, Joseph tells the king the dream, gives him the interpretation, and overnight, he becomes second in command of the kingdom. The king said, "You have something because none of my magicians could tell me the dream." They thought it was unfair. They said, "We can tell you what it means, but tell us what it is. You have to be fair." Joseph did not need to know the dream and that is a sign to us of God's presence being with him because of purity and cleanness of heart.

God Wants Purity of Heart!
The Devil Hates Purity Because
He Knows You Will Have God's Glory

God wants purity of heart and the devil wants to make you unclean, so you will not have God's power and glory. More than ever before, we are living in that day we need to be walking as clean vessels. We are not running all over the place trying to figure this thing out. It is simple; God is looking for pure vessels.

What it comes down to is this. Right now for purity, are we willing to have that time of intimacy with God, and let that sound of purity come out of us? That sound of purity will come out of our dance, worship, and prayer. That sound of purity will come out of your spirit and preaching, and the purity and cleanness will pierce the darkness.

The devil hates to stand before God in the presence of purity. He hates it. That is the reason the devil wants to defile a vessel quickly. As soon as young girls and boys get of age, he wants to defile them. Even before they get of age, he wants to defile the temple so that it is unholy to God. He wants to defile the temple quickly.

The Power of Intense Prayer, Purity, Passion & Emptying Self

"Like the prophet Jeremiah, Charles G. Finney was anointed of God to "root out" and to "plant" in the Lord's vineyard, (Jer. 1:10). He was a man of intense prayer, purity, and passion. 'Emptied of self, he was filled with the Holy Spirit.' His sermons were chain lightning, flashing conviction into the hearts of the stoutest skeptics. Simple as a child in his utterances, he sometimes startled his hearers by his unique prayers. He could thunder the judgments of God upon sin with great liberty and power and then offer the mercy of the gospel with tenderness and tears. Without question, he was a prophetic voice to 19th century America. His ministry consistently produced revivals, even in areas considered hardened and unreceptive to the gospel. Finney's autobiography is filled with accounts of powerful manifestations of the Spirit."[3]

"Finney seems to have had the power of impressing the conscience of men with the necessity of holy living in such a manner as produced lasting results. 'Over eighty-five in every hundred person professing conversion to Christ in Finney's meetings remained true to God. Whereas seventy percent of those professing Christ in meetings of even so great an evangelist as Moody afterward became backsliders.' Such results were the fruit of hours and hours of prayer. It was not Finney's prayers alone that secured such heaven sent revivals. Finney's was supported by the prayers of two of God's hidden treasures. It was the hidden, yet powerful intercessions of "Father Nash" and Abel Clary that laid the groundwork for these mighty moves of God."[4]

Price for the Glory

God's light and glory will shine out of you to bring freedom to others when you do these things to keep a pure and clean heart. *"Remove the heavy yoke of oppression. Stop pointing your finger and spreading vicious rumors! Feed the hungry, and help those in trouble. Then your light will shine out from the darkness ..."* (Isaiah 58:9-10a NLT).

After you have a clean heart and do these things, then your light will shine out from the darkness. It does not matter how dark it is right now. He says, *"... and the darkness around you will be as bright as noon"* (Isaiah 58:10b). Your light will shine out from the darkness! When folks get around you and they have uncleanness and things of darkness, God says that the darkness around you will be bright as noon. It will be so bright! "Breakthrough" is another word for that. You are having a breakthrough when your light shines out of darkness and the darkness around you is bright as noon. That is breakthrough!

The light is breaking through; it is another dimension. Breakthrough is happening in your life. It does not matter how dark it is, the light will break forth. It does not matter how feeble or impossible it looks, your light will break forth.

For the sake of breakthrough, Jesus said, "I'm going to

fast, but when I leave, my disciples will fast. They are going to fast while I am gone. So much is going to happen inside of them. Then, wherever they go, they will bring a breakthrough." God's breakthrough is not like your breakthrough because godliness will lead you forward. This is your season for breakthrough!

The drier you are, the greater your breakthrough. *"The LORD will guide you continually, giving you water when you are dry and restoring your strength ..."* (Isaiah 58:11 NLT). It sounds so simple, but the drier you are, the greater the hand of God will move in your life. The drier you are, the greater that God can come in and sweep the place, when you cry out to God with complete surrender of your heart to love on Him with hunger to be filled with His presence, and drink from His life-giving water.

A breakthrough came on the woman in the Bible who came to Jesus, knelt down at His feet, and began to take her hair and wash His feet. She humbled herself with full surrender of her heart and loved Him because she treasured His love and presence more than anything else in this world. People were upset with her and He said, "He that has been forgiven much, loves so much." *"I tell you, her sins—and they are many—have been forgiven, so she has shown me much love. But a person who is forgiven little shows only little love"* (Luke 7:47 NLT).

Breakthrough came to this woman. In that scripture, Jesus was talking about how much she has been forgiven because of her greater degree of love. Some people do not recognize that they have been forgiven and how much they have been forgiven. Therefore, they do not have great love. However, a person that recognizes how much they have been forgiven is one that has great love. Breakthrough happens when you give Him all your love and He floods you with His great love.

The same thing happens if you are dry. When you know you do not have it altogether, and the drier you are in that place, as you cry out to God, breakthrough happens. When you depend on God because you cannot do it, you will have greater results, stirring, satisfaction, and the greatest praise. On the contrary, there are people who think that they have it all together, and can do it with their own ability and without His presence.

If we are dry and cry out, "God, I'm in a dry place. I need you," God said, "The Lord your God will give you water when you are dry and will restore your strength." When you draw from the river of God's glory, *"... You will be like a well-watered garden like an ever flowing spring"* (Isaiah 58:11 NLT). In order words, God is talking about light breaking forth, out of the darkness. He is talking about a well-watered garden coming out of dryness. That is breakthrough! That is the glory breaking through!

Afterwards, He will build you up because He is saying that it is not just for you to experience Him, but He is getting ready to rebuild some homes and reestablish some things. *"Some of you will rebuild the deserted ruins of your cities. Then you will be known as a rebuilder of walls and a restorer of homes"* (Isaiah 58:12 NLT). He is going to transform some communities. He is going to make some things happen because you went into that place with Him. Intimacy in God brings revival!

Once you are in that place with God, then you allow God to do the overhaul in you. I love what Charles Finney prayed; he prayed that the Lord would do an overhaul in him. He let God overhaul his temple. He spent a whole season in prayer where his mind was deeply exercised in that area of personal holiness. That means that in his time of prayer, this was the only thing on his mind. It was this issue of personal holiness!

A Right Spirit Seeks
To Know God's Ways

Today, as you grow more intimate with God, you can carry the spirit of revival and the spirit of what I am speaking. God might have given you an assignment and it is supposed to impact people, but maybe you have not done it yet, because you are waiting to see who is going with you. Maybe you are waiting to see who is going in there with you or who is seeing it with you. Having the right spirit to seek God's ways and presence is most important and this is something that happens between you and God.

Seeking to know God's ways is another level that most believers do not practice. Moses said, "Lord, I haven't gone yet, because you haven't told me who you will send with me." The scripture says, *"One day Moses said to the LORD, But you haven't told me whom you will send with me. You have been telling me, take these people up to the Promised Land. But you haven't told me, whom you will send with me. You have told me, I know you by name, and I look favorably on you. If it is true that you look favorably on me, let me know your ways ... "* (Exodus 33:12-13 NLT).

Many do not have this desire and hunger to know God's ways and understand Him more fully. They know God by what He can do for them and they are content with it— they are fine and happy. They are content if God can fix their problem to get them out of it, or get them a certain job, and they seek Him for the things He can do for them.

Moses went to another place in God. This same man saw the waters divide (Exodus chapter 14). God even told him to stop crying out to Him. Literally, "Stop praying. Lift up your hands and begin to see the hand of God move." In other words, "Moses get up and get going!"

Sometimes, you can pray in doubt and not truly believe. Moses came to the place where he saw the hand of God. He said to Moses, "Stop crying, get up, lift up your hands, and divide the Red Sea!" He did not say to lift his hands and when Moses did, God would divide the Red Sea. Instead, He said, "Lift up your hands and you divide the Red Sea!" If he had not lifted up his hands, the Red Sea would not have parted.

God is trying to move you to that place that He is waiting for you to hear Him say, "Lift up your hands and divide the Red Sea." The reason it has not parted is that you have not lifted up your hands yet. If you are not hearing the voice of God and think it is going to be fixed another way, the only way you can have a powerful move of God is to do it His way. Moses did it God's way and God did His part.

When Moses obeyed to do his part, then God did His part. All night, God caused the wind to blow until the land was dry. When he was standing there trapped, the Bible says that cloud began to circle around the children of Israel and protected the rear of the children of Israel. It came in a pillar of fire and God was moving all night long, keeping the enemy from the children of Israel. They did not even have to worry about it. God was protecting them.

Likewise, when you do it God's way, you will not have to worry. This is what happens when your godliness leads you; God will protect you from behind. Like Moses, if you have a right spirit to seek His glory, you will not have to focus on your problems and things. Keeping your heart right is all you need to do for godliness to lead you and then, God will protect you.

In correlation with that, your focus must be on keeping purity in your heart so that you become pure vessels. Then, you will not worry about those attacks from the rear that you cannot stop anyway. God's pillar of fire is the only thing that will be able to stop those attacks that you cannot stop.

With Moses, God was the only one that Pharaoh could not stop. Pharaoh could do nothing against His glory. That water parted all night, and then God released it at the right time to destroy the enemy.

Here is the key to knowing God's ways. I want to live in such a way that God is my rear guard! Moses is saying to God, "Right now, I want to know your ways!" In other words, "Take me into this place now! I want to know how you think! I want to know how you respond to thing! I want to know how you judge! I want to know your desires! I want to know how you live!" *"If it is true that you look favorably on me, let me know your ways ..."* (Exodus 33:13 NLT).

That is another level—that is another place. He had already seen the mighty hand of God, but now he is talking to God in another way—a new level of intimacy!

If God does not reveal it to us, we will not even know it. This is what Moses was saying. "I want to know your ways!" With most people that we know, they may not want to know God that way and just want God to fix things.

However, Moses had a different spirit. He sought to know the way God thinks and lives, and he sought His desires and responses. This is the right spirit you must have and is what God wants before He can make Himself strong in and through you!

A Right Spirit Seeks to Know God
To Understand God More Fully

When you have a right spirit, you hunger to know God's

ways so that you can understand God more fully. *"... let me know your ways so I may understand you more fully ..."* (Exodus 33:13 NLT). This is what Moses is saying to God. "I want to know your ways!" In other words, "I saw how awesome your hand is, but I do not understand you." God said He would harden the heart of Pharaoh so that He might show His glory. Likewise, you need to know that God will harden the heart of people that are against you so that He might show His glory through you.

Intentionally, He hardened the heart of Pharaoh so that He might show His glory. Some may have been thinking that He is going to make Pharaoh's heart soft so that it would be well with us. Then God says, "No, that's what you want. What I want is that I'm going to harden his heart so that all of Egypt will know that there is a God in Israel." *Intimacy in God* will allow us to know His secrets and thoughts.

A Right Spirit Seeks To Know God
For the Sake of Obedience
And to Enjoy His Favor

When you have a right spirit, you will hunger to know God's ways so that you can obey Him and enjoy His favor. *"... let me know your ways so I may understand you more fully and continue to enjoy your favor ..."* (Exodus 33:13 NLT). Moses understood that if he knew God's ways, favor would be on his life. For this reason, he only wanted to know God's ways with the purpose to do them and that is what pleased God.

In contrast to the spirit that Moses had, many people just want to know about God, but they do not plan to do what He says. They do not plan to live it. They only want greater knowledge, but not necessarily to have greater understanding. As a result, they struggle to hear and obey

God. There are times we can get so busy trying to give someone a word, but God has already spoken to that person and he or she is not listening. Obedience is always better than any sacrifice!

On the other hand, God may be speaking to you and He cannot get you to obey, but yet, you can hear Him clearly for someone else.

To have God's glory and favor, it is more important that you obey God by putting Him first place in your life. That should be your greatest desire.

Like Moses, we should desire to be tender enough to hear the Word of God, and when it comes to us, we will obey it.

Coupled with that, Moses tied something together. He was following God so much that he said, "Wait a minute God; if I know your ways, I will be able to see you more fully, so that I will want to do what you say. I understand that there is favor that moves on my life when I obey you." Moses asked God to show him those things and the Lord told him that He would personally go with him.

The scripture says it this way, *"'... And remember that this nation is your very own people.' The LORD replied, 'I will personally go with you, Moses, and I will give you rest— everything will be fine for you'"* (Exodus 33:13-14 NLT). That is a wonderful promise of God's favor!

In other words, Moses is asking, "Lord, you're telling me to do something, but who's going to go with me? Who's going to stand with me?" Then, God turns around and says, "I will personally go with you. Rest, everything is going to be fine." In essence, that is favor and God will do the same for you, and respond when you seek to know His ways and have His presence in your life.

God's Presence is the Only Thing
That Sets You Apart From Others

When you go after His Glory, His presence is the only thing that sets you apart. If God's presence is not in your life, then in the people's eyes, nothing separates you from them. One can talk about the kind of Christian he is, what church he attends and with whom he is associated; but if people do not see the glory and presence of God, they feel like that person does not have anything. *"Then Moses said, 'If you don't personally go with us, don't make us leave this place. How will anyone know that you look favorably on me—on me and on your people—if you don't go with us? For your presence among us sets your people and me apart from all other people on the earth'"* (Exodus 33:15-16 NLT).

The presence of God separates God's people from the people of the earth. His glory is the number one thing that you ought to be going after; that is what separates you from all of His people. Your title does not matter. If people do not see that we carry the glory, they see that we are no different from them. Then, we are just a person that has a title. They can see whether you carry God's presence.

Sinners will tell you this if you are no different from them. When you are not living right, they are going to tell it. Some of them will ask you if you are going to the club tonight. You may have already told them that you are saved. Nevertheless, they will ask if you are going to the club with them and act as if you never even said a word. They do not believe that you are different from them because they do not see any glory.

To sum it up, the glory led the children of Israel. It made the difference and set them apart from others. They did not have the Holy Spirit inside them, as we do. Everywhere they went, they had to follow the glory. When the glory stopped, they had to rest. If it stayed three weeks, four weeks, or six weeks, it did not matter. Until that glory got up and began to lead, they stayed in the desert. As soon as the glory began to move, they picked up their tents, and everything else and began to move. They did not know where they were going, and to follow the glory was the only thing they could do!

Go After God's Glory With Utmost Respect & His Abiding Goodness Will Favor You

You must go after God's glory with the utmost respect and like Moses, you can have God's favor. When you ask God something, He will respond. You need to live in such a way that God will tell you, "I will indeed do what you asked." He said, "I look favorably on you. When you ask me something, I'm going to act; I'm going to respond." This is what God told Moses, *"The LORD replied to Moses, 'I will indeed do what you have asked for I look favorably on you, and I know you by name.' Moses responded, 'Then show me your glorious presence'"* (Exodus 33:17-18 NLT).

After God said that He would look favorably on him, Moses said, *"Then show me your glory."* He just had the promise. God said, "If you ask me, I will act; I'm going to be with you and everything is going to be fine." Moses took advantage of it and said, *"Then show me your glory."* He did not go after houses, land, and things, but seeing God's glory was the upmost important thing in his life.

Likewise, in the same manner, we need to go after the glory with the same attitude, honor, and respect. Moses went after the treasure of Heaven. He went after something he could not get anywhere else and only God could give it to him. When Moses said, *"Show me the glory,"* and he desired to go after it, this moved the heart of God.

134

More than anything, we need to ask God to show us His glory so that we can obey Him. This is the first time in the Bible that we read where a man asked God to show him the glory. Of all the men that lived before him, he was the first one that ever said, *"Show me your glory."* That is another level and this means that we desire God to pull us into another place, and show us how He lives, walks, and talks.

When you ask God to show you His glory, He will respond and make His goodness pass before you. This is how God responded to Moses after he asked Him to show him His glory; *"The LORD replied, I will make all my goodness pass before you ..."* (Exodus 33:19 NLT).

God showed him His goodness. When you ask God to show you His glory, God will let you see His goodness. Everything in the glory is good; everything that comes out of the glory is good. When he says, "God show me your glory." God says, "I'll show you my goodness!"

To put it differently, this means that when you walk in the glory of God, you are covered in His goodness; everything is coming out of His glory. It does not matter what is happening in your life, everything that comes out of the glory is good.

When Adam lived with God, he lived with God's goodness. In the end time, when you are living with God, you are living in His goodness. Everything that comes out of the glory is goodness. That is why He clothes you in and with His glory.

Do you want healing? It comes out of the glory. Do you want deliverance? It comes out of the glory. Do you need to be lifted up? It comes out of the glory. As a vessel that carries God's glory when you minister to people, even though you do not know what they need, as you do your part,

God does His part. That is because His goodness comes out of you. It is God's desire for us to live in the glory, and God is saying, "Just do your part, and live."

Not only will God's goodness go before you, but also, God said He would call out His name. *"The LORD replied, 'I will make all my goodness pass before you, and I will call out my name ...'"* (Exodus 33:19 NLT). God says, "I'm going to show you my glory and call out my own name." It is one thing for us to call out His name, but it is another thing for Him to call out His own name.

Prayer to Know God & be Filled
With His Holiness & Glory

"Heavenly Father, you are too much to contain. You are too much to handle! Your Word and presence melts my heart. I am like dishcloth in your presence. You have melted my heart. You are too much to understand, but I know that I want your glory.

"Just like Moses, I want it. I know I want it. Father, hear my cry. I don't know it, but I want it. I want to know your ways. I want to know how you live, walk, and talk. I want to have an intimate relationship with you. Show me your glory, Father. Lord, do an overhaul in me and fill me with your holiness so I can obey you. My only reason for prayer is that I keep my heart right with you, and be filled with your holiness. Fill me with your holiness, Lord!

"Draw me with intense hunger to pray, even when I am dry, and that I might take time away from my busy schedule to go after your presence, and put you first place in my life. I yield myself to you because I want your holiness, Lord! You are my greatest delight! And, I want to pray with only one purpose to be in that place with you. I delight in you and your presence more than any other person or thing on earth. I love you Lord. You are my delight! Take me into this place with you God, I want to know how you think. I want to know how you respond to things. I want to know your desires and responses. I want to know how you live. I just want to know you, Lord. That is my greatest hunger and intimacy in you.

"I yield myself to you because I am going after your Glory. I thank you for your glory. Your presence is the only thing that sets me apart from others and the world. Your glory is the number one thing that I am going after. Nothing else is more valuable to me than to go after your godliness and glory, which are the treasures of Heaven. I know that I can't make it without your glory. I am desperate for you Lord. I want your glory because I know that without your glory, people won't be saved unless they see your name exalted by the demonstration of your power and presence that they can feel and see.

"Change my heart Lord and fill me with your godliness that will lead me so I can obey you. Lord, I want to be led by your godliness. I know that your protection and covering keeps me safe when I follow you, and I am not led by what I think. I surrender my desires, will, ways, thoughts, plans, and motives to you, Lord. Not my will be done, but yours, Lord. I thank you Jesus for all of this and I give you praise for doing it. Amen."

Conclusion

In conclusion, I challenge you to focus on your intimacy in God by never allowing anything or any person to stop you from going after God's presence and glory as the upmost desire in your life. Let prayer be a daily and continual surrender of your heart as you get in the inner place, and stay there until you are changed and filled with His presence.

You can be a carrier of God's abiding presence and supernatural glory with demonstration of power continually flowing in and through you to bring people to Jesus! As you have read in this book, it comes with the price of having a right heart, purity, holiness, and godliness of heart in prayer, and living it out in your daily life.

You can have God's presence so real that His presence sets you apart from others. Most of all, it is God's heart that you would allow these truths to be applied in your heart as you pray to know God and be filled with His Holiness.

Keep your heart clean, focused on purity, and the baptism of purity. Let this be your priority as you are in prayer, and all things you do in life. In your intimacy with God, He will teach you how to listen to His voice and follow His Spirit. Never stop yielding to God and His Word. Not only intimacy with God, but also *intimacy in God* is my prayer for you. May He alone be your all and all!

In everything you do, you are building God's house, a place for Him to dwell in your heart. Never quit staying in His presence. Tell the world what Jesus has done for you and His power and glorious presence will come on them as it comes on you with intimacy in God.

ENDNOTES

1. Webster's New World Dictionary, Third College Addition, New World Dictionary, a division of Simon & Schuster, Inc., a major revision of Webster's New World Dictionary, Second College Addition, 1985 & 1970, 1972, 1974, 1976, 1978, 1979, 1080, 1982, and 1984 by Simon & Schuster, Inc., pp. 1091.
2. ibid.
3. Awake And Go! Global Prayer Network. Website Article "Charles G. Finney" written by David Smithers www.watchword.org/index.
4. ibid.

ABOUT
THE AUTHOR

Bishop Glenn Collier serves his congregation, *New Harvester International Ministries,* in Dacula, Georgia, as founder and senior pastor, and as a bishop with the *Fellowship of International Churches.* He has been a speaker on *Preach the Word,* Worldwide TV Network, and featured guest on *The Gospel Touch Show,* TV 57 WATC Atlanta.

Bishop Collier has over 25 years of ministry experience being involved in all aspects of ministry from church planting and prison ministry, to directing men's ministry and evangelism. Because of his passion to see others raised up to fulfill their God given purpose, he has become a spiritual father to many.

He has a tremendous heart for intimate worship with a passion and anointing for provoking, challenging, and encouraging people to reach their full potential in life and in God. Often, as he preaches, the Lord releases a greater hunger and passion for God's Word, His presence, and personal revival. Many times, while ministering, people are significantly touched in their hearts with manifest weeping and brokenness before God, as the Holy Spirit comes in power. The presence and power of the Holy Spirit moves people into more committed and consecrated lives, while strengthening many towards their divine purpose in God.

Bishop Collier and his beautiful wife Linda Collier have been married over 30 years and the Lord has greatly blessed them with six children, four grandchildren and many spiritual sons and daughters.